HAPPY BIRTHDAY, WANDA JUNE

BOOKS BY KURT VONNEGUT, JR.

PLAYER PIANO

THE SIRENS OF TITAN

MOTHER NIGHT

CANARY IN A CATHOUSE

CAT'S CRADLE

GOD BLESS YOU, MR. ROSEWATER

WELCOME TO THE MONKEY HOUSE

SLAUGHTERHOUSE-FIVE

HAPPY BIRTHDAY, WANDA JUNE

A PLAY BY

Kurt Vonnegut, Jr.

HAPPY BIRTHDAY, WANDA JUNE

A DELTA BOOK

A DELTA BOOK
Published by
Dell Publishing Co., Inc.
750 Third Avenue, New York, N. Y. 10017

Delta ® TM 755118, Dell Publishing Co., Inc.
Reprinted by arrangement with Delacorte Press
A Seymour Lawrence Book, New York
Manufactured in the United States of America
First Delta printing—September 1971

The pictures on pages v, xi, xiii, xv, xvi, 54,
104, 114, 125, 134, 148, and 171 are by Jill Krementz.
Those on pages 60 and 68 are by Bert Andrews.

Designed by Joel Schick

ABOUT THIS PLAY

This play is what I did when I was forty-seven years old—when my six children were children no more. It was a time of change, of good-bye and good-bye and good-bye. My big house was becoming a museum of vanished childhoods—of my vanished young manhood as well.

This was on Cape Cod. There were widows all around me—in houses like mine.

I was drinking more and arguing a lot, and I had to get out of that house.

I was supposedly a right-handed person, but I found myself using my left hand more and more. It became the hand that did most of the giving and taking for me. I asked my older brother what he knew about this. He said that I had been an ambidextrous infant. I had been *taught* to favor my right hand.

"I'm left-handed now, and I'm through with novels," I told him. "I'm writing a play. It's plays from now on."

I was writing myself a new family and a new early manhood. I was going to fool myself, and spooks in a novel couldn't do the job. I had to hire actors—pay them to say what I wished them to say, to dress as I wished them to dress, to laugh, to cry, to come or go when I said to.

Strictly speaking, I was rewriting an old play of mine. But that old play had been written by a right-handed stranger fifteen years my junior.

Fifteen years ago my wife and I conducted a Great Books program on Cape Cod. And when we read and discussed *The Odyssey,* the behavior of Odysseus at his homecoming struck me as cruelly preposterous. So I wrote a play about it, which I called *Penelope.*

Ernest Hemingway was still alive and seemingly well. So I felt free to imagine a modern Odysseus who was a lot like that part of Hemingway which I detested—the slayer of nearly extinct animals which meant him no harm.

The play was performed for one week at the Orleans Arena Theatre on the Cape. Harold Ryan, the hero, had a line in that version which went like this: "Things die. All things die." After the play closed at Orleans, I said that to my wife, and I returned to writing short stories and novels.

As a footnote to American theatrical history: the Orleans Arena Theatre, run by Gordon and Betsy Argo, produced six new plays by unknown writers, with no financial help from anyone.

During that same year, the Ford Foundation underwrote the production of ten new plays—at a cost of a hundred thousand dollars or more.

The Argos lost something like three hundred and nineteen dollars that year. So it goes.

Penelope, which became *Happy Birthday, Wanda June,* has been around so long that it was once optioned by Estelle Parsons—before she decided to be an actress. Think of that. Estelle used to suppose that she would be a producer some day.

She failed to produce *Penelope* for this reason: it was

a lousy play. Actors complained that there were no parts for stars, that everybody got to talk as much as everybody else, that nobody changed or was proved right or wrong at the end.

This intolerable balancing of characters and arguments reflected my true feelings: I felt and I still feel that everybody is right, no matter what he says. I had, in fact, written a book about everybody's being right all the time, *The Sirens of Titan.* And I gave a name in that book to a mathematical point where all opinions, no matter how contradictory, harmonized. I called it a *chrono-synclastic infundibulum.*

I live in one.

Somewhere in there my father died, and one of the last things he said to me was that I had never written a story with a villain in it. That was surely one of the troubles with my play—and that remains a major trouble with it to this day. Even after we opened *Happy Birthday, Wanda June,* we experimented shamelessly with endings. We had various people shoot Harold, including children. We had Harold shoot various people, including children. We had Harold do the world the favor of shooting himself.

Nothing satisfied, and I am persuaded that nothing could satisfy, since the author did not have the balls to make Harold or anybody thoroughly vile.

That was chickenhearted of me. It was Edgar Lee Masters' *Spoon River Anthology,* and some other things, which has made me chickenhearted about villainy. I marveled at all the epitaphs in Masters' book when I was only twelve years old, and I was bound to say to myself, "My gosh—all those people *had* to be what they were."

My father and mother also tended to make me chickenhearted. My father was a frail architect and painter. He was also a gun nut, which used to amaze me. It seemed so inharmonious with the rest of him, that he should fondle guns.

He left me some guns.

My two siblings didn't like his gunplay, either. One time, I remember, my brother looked at a quail Father had shot, and he said, "My gosh—that's like smashing a fine Swiss watch." My sister used to cry and refuse to eat when Father brought home game.

Some homecoming for Odysseus!

Lester Goldsmith produced my play. He had never produced a play before. He used to be an executive at Paramount Pictures. And then he became an independent producer of political films. We met in the spring of 1970, at the home of Don Farber, who was a lawyer for both of us.

Lester remembered having read a synopsis of *Penelope,* which my agents had circulated around Hollywood years before. After we'd all had a few drinks, he said, "I'll option that play."

Which he did. And I went home and rewrote it all summer long.

Lester and I were inspired amateurs where legitimate theater was concerned. We remain good friends. God willing, we'll produce more plays less amateurishly.

Lester hired a theater before we had a script. And he moved so quickly that we needed a director almost immediately. No New York director was willing to take the

job without a finished script in hand. What I had to
show at that point, two months before opening night, was
a filthy tossed salad of corrasable bond.

A television director from the West Coast examined
the tossed salad. He was a good man who had directed
such gruesome enterprises as *Gilligan's Island* and
The Art Linkletter Show. He had done a lot of little
theater, too, and had as his happiest memories the days
when he had been the director of the road company
of *Mr. Roberts*. His name was Michael J. Kane.

Mike and I must have come within a few hundred yards
of each other in 1949 or so, when I saw his production
of *Mr. Roberts* in Schenectady, New York. I was a public
relations man at the time. That was where I learned my
nice manners—as a public relations man.

I told Mike, when we met in New York City, that I
had seen his show so long ago. We were nearly the same
age, and he was so deep into remembering his youth
that he said to me, without any hesitation, "Schenectady!
My God how it snowed!"

He agreed to direct *Happy Birthday, Wanda June*. He
was running away from home and some other
things—for a little while. So was I. So was Lester.

It is my opinion that the writer and the producer and the
director were pleasant, enthusiastic fools about theater.
But Mike assembled a cast, headed by Kevin McCarthy,
which was the equal of any cast in New York. Eliot
Norton, the Boston critic, told me in conversation that
our actors worked together as excitingly as Englishmen.
High praise! I said of them, toward the end, "They're like
The Harlem Globetrotters! Look at 'em go!"

The main trouble was with the author, who didn't

really know what he was doing—except running away from home. There I was: all alone in a tiny penthouse borrowed from a friend, six doors down and fifteen floors up from the Theatre de Lys, where the actors were rehearsing. I was writing new beginnings and middles and ends. My nice manners and neat appearance decayed. I came to resemble a madman who was attempting to extract moonbeams from excrement.

We opened on October 7, 1970, at the de Lys. The reviews were mixed, as they say. We had actors, but no play—or, worse, we had an awfully long, old-fashioned play with no ending. We kept running, though.

And I kept rewriting. I became pathologically suggestible. If somebody had told me to paint my feet blue for the sake of the play, I would have done it solemnly. Blue-footed, I would have asked Lester to do what I was always asking him, "All right—we're ready. Invite Clive Barnes and John Simon to have another look." I would do anything anybody told me to do—but go home.

I now thank heaven that my main advisors were the actors, my new family. Their advice, particularly Kevin McCarthy's advice, was expert and beautiful. I was still rewriting six weeks after we opened. And along came an off-Broadway actors' strike.

So we tottered uptown to the Edison Theatre, and opened again. We closed there on March 14, 1971, after 142 performances. There was standing room only at the final performance, a Sunday matinee. Some good soul shouted, "Bravo!" The actors had saved the play.

Things die. All things die. My new family dissolved into the late afternoon. As we went our separate ways out of the theater district, blue movies and peepshows

offered to confirm our new solitude, if we cared
to drop in.

Walking home along Forty-seventh Street, I remembered
having asked Kevin and Nick Coster and Marsha
Mason what the end would be like. This was during
supper at Duff's, shortly after rehearsals had begun. "Does
being in a play with a person often make that person
a friend for life?" I said.

"You'd think it would—and I always think it will,"
said Nick.

"When a play closes," said Marsha, "everybody
promises everybody else that they will go on seeing a lot
of each other. . . ." She paused to remember the closings
she had endured.

Kevin finished the thought for her brusquely,
unsentimentally, in the manner of Ernest Hemingway.
"But they *don't*," he said. He took an iron-jawed bite of
hot bread with garlic butter. The subject was closed.

Here is who the members of my new family were—and
I list them in the order of their appearance in our
posters and ads:

KEVIN McCARTHY—Harold Ryan

KEITH CHARLES—Dr. Norbert Woodly

NICOLAS COSTER—Herb Shuttle

WILLIAM HICKEY—Col. Looseleaf Harper

MARSHA MASON—Penelope Ryan

LOUIS TURENNE—Siegfried von Konigswald

STEVEN PAUL—Paul Ryan

ARIANE MUNKER—Wanda June

ELLEN DANO—Wanda June (After Ariane became exhausted)

PAMELA SAUNDERS—Mildred Ryan

JESS OSUNA—Understudy for all the men
DIANE WIEST—Understudy for both women

Both understudies got on, and brought with them exciting
new stuff.

ED WITTSTEIN—Settings
DAVID F. SEGAL—Lighting
JOSEPH G. AULISI—Costumes
GARY HARRIS—Sound
WALTER ROSEN SCHOLZ—Associate Producer
PAUL JOHN AUSTIN—Stage Manager

Auf wiedersehen!

HAPPY BIRTHDAY, WANDA JUNE

CAST

PENELOPE RYAN, 30

PAUL RYAN, 12, her son

HAROLD RYAN, 55, her husband

COLONEL LOOSELEAF HARPER, 50,
  her husband's sidekick

HERB SHUTTLE, 35, a suitor

DR. NORBERT WOODLY, 35, a suitor

WANDA JUNE, 10, a ghost

MAJOR SIEGFRIED VON KONIGSWALD, 50,
  a German ghost

MILDRED, 45, Harold's former wife, a ghost

ACT ONE

SCENE ONE

SILENCE.   Pitch blackness. Animal
eyes begin to glow in the darkness.
Sounds of the jungle climax in animals
fighting. A SINGER is heard singing the
first bars of "All God's Chillun Got
Shoes." HAROLD, LOOSELEAF,
PENELOPE, and WOODLY stand in a row
in the darkness, facing the audience.
They are motionless. A city skyline in
the early evening materializes outside
the windows.

The lights come up on the living
room of a rich man's apartment, which
is densely furnished with trophies of
hunts and wars. There is a front door,
a door to the master bedroom suite,
and a corridor leading to other
bedrooms, the kitchen and so on.

PENELOPE
How do you do. My name is Penelope Ryan. This is a
simple-minded play about men who enjoy killing—and
those who don't.

HAROLD
I am Harold Ryan, her husband. I have killed perhaps
two hundred men in wars of various sorts—as a
professional soldier. I have killed thousands of other
animals as well—for sport.

WOODLY
I am Dr. Norbert Woodly—a physician, a healer. I find it
disgusting and frightening that a killer should still be a
respected member of society. Gentleness must replace
violence everywhere, or we are doomed.

PENELOPE

[*To* LOOSELEAF]

Would you like to say something about killing, Colonel?

LOOSELEAF

[*Embarrassed*]

Jesus—I dunno. You know. What the heck. Who knows?

PENELOPE
Colonel Harper, retired now, dropped an atom bomb
on Nagasaki during the Second World War, killing
seventy-four thousand people in a flash.

LOOSELEAF
I dunno, boy.

PENELOPE
You don't *know?*

LOOSELEAF
It was a bitch.

PENELOPE
Thank you.

   [*To all*]

You can leave now. We'll begin.

WOODLY

   [*To the audience, making a peace sign*]

Peace!

   [*All but* PENELOPE *exit*]

PENELOPE

   [*To the audience*]

This is a tragedy. When it's done, my face will be as white as the snows of Kilimanjaro.

   [*Hyena laughs*]

My husband, who kills so much, has been missing for eight years. He disappeared in a light plane over the

Amazon Rain Forest, where he hoped to find diamonds as
big as cantaloupes. His pilot was Colonel Looseleaf
Harper, who dropped the bomb on Nagasaki.

[*Hyena laughs*]

I should explain the doorbells in this apartment. They
were built by Abercrombie and Fitch. They are actual
recordings of animal cries. The back doorbell is a hyena,
which you've just heard. The front doorbell is a lion's roar.

[*To the wings*]

Would you let them hear it please?

[*Lion roars*]

Thank you.

[PAUL, *her twelve-year-old son, enters from corridor,
a sensitive, neatly dressed little rich boy*]

And this is my son, Paul. He was only four years old
when his father disappeared.

PAUL

[*Radiantly, sappily*]

He's coming back, Mom! He's the bravest, most wonderful
man who ever lived.

PENELOPE

[*To audience*]

I told you this was a simple-minded play.

PAUL
Maybe he'll come back tonight! It's his birthday.

PENELOPE
I know.

PAUL
Stay home tonight!

PENELOPE

[*Ruefully, for they have been over this before*]

Oh, Paul—

PAUL
You're married! You've already got a husband!

PENELOPE
He's a ghost!

PAUL
He's alive!

PENELOPE
Not even Mutual of Omaha thinks so anymore.

PAUL

If you have to go out with some guy—can't he be more like Dad?

[*Sick*]

Herb Shuttle and Norbert Woodly—can't you do better than those two freaks?

PENELOPE

[*Resentfully*]

Thank you, kind sir.

PAUL

A vacuum cleaner salesman and a fairy doctor.

PENELOPE

A *what* kind of doctor?

PAUL

A fairy—a queer. Everybody in the building knows he's a queer.

PENELOPE

[*Knowing better*]

That's an interesting piece of news.

PAUL

You're the only woman he ever took out.

PENELOPE
Not true.

PAUL
Still lives with his mother.

PENELOPE
You know she has no *feet!* You want him to abandon his mother, who has no husband, who has no money of her own, who has no feet?

PAUL
How did she lose her feet?

PENELOPE
In a railroad accident many years ago.

PAUL
I was afraid to ask.

PENELOPE
Norbert was just beginning practice. A real man would have sold her to a catfood company, I suppose. As far as that goes, J. Edgar Hoover still lives with his mother.

PAUL
I didn't know that.

PENELOPE
A lot of people don't.

PAUL
J. Edgar Hoover plays sports.

PENELOPE
I don't really know.

PAUL
The only exercise Dr. Woodly ever gets is playing the violin and making that stupid peace sign.

[*He makes the peace sign and says the word effeminately*]

Peace. Peace. Peace, everybody.

[*Lion doorbell roars*]

PENELOPE

[*Cringing*]

I hate that thing.

PAUL
It's beautiful.

[*He goes to door, admits* WOODLY, *whom he loathes openly*]

WOODLY

[*Wearing street clothes, carrying a rolled-up poster under his arm*]

Peace, everybody—Paul, Penelope.

PAUL
You're taking Mom out tonight?

WOODLY

[*To* PENELOPE]

You're going out?

PENELOPE
Herb Shuttle is taking me to a fight.

WOODLY
Take plenty of cigars.

PENELOPE

[*An apology, secret from* PAUL]

We made the date three months ago.

WOODLY
I must take you to an emergency ward sometime—on a Saturday night. That's also fun. I came to see Selma, as a matter of fact.

PENELOPE
She quit this afternoon.

PAUL
We don't have a maid any more.

WOODLY
Oh?

PENELOPE
The animals made her sneeze and cry too much.

WOODLY
I'm glad somebody finally cried. Every time I come in here and see all this unnecessary death, *I* want to cry.

[*Winking at* PAUL, *acknowledging* PAUL's *low opinion of him*]

I don't cry, of course. Not manly, you know. Did she try antihistamines?

PENELOPE
They made her so sleepy she couldn't work.

WOODLY
Throw out all this junk. Burn it! This room crawls with tropical disease.

PAUL
Everything stays as it is!

WOODLY
A monument to a man who thought that what the world needed most was more rhinoceros meat.

PAUL

[*Hotly*]

My father!

WOODLY
I apologize. But you didn't know him, and neither did I.
How's your asthma?

PAUL
Don't worry about it.

WOODLY
How's the fungus around your thumbnail?

PAUL

[*Concealing the thumb*]

It's fine!

WOODLY
It's jungle rot! This room is making everybody sick! This
is your family doctor speaking now.

[*Unrolling the poster*]

Here—I brought you something else to hang on your wall,
for the sake of variety.

PENELOPE

[*Reading*]

"War is not healthy for children and other living things."
How lovely.

WOODLY
No doubt Paul thinks it stinks.

[*Lion doorbell roars*]

I hate that thing.

PAUL

[*Going to the door*]

Keeps fairies away!

[*He admits* HERB SHUTTLE, *who carries an Electrolux vacuum cleaner*]

SHUTTLE

[*To* PAUL *affectionately, touching him*]

Hi kid.

[*Seeing* WOODLY]

Would you look what the cat dragged in.

WOODLY
I'm glad you brought your vacuum cleaner.

SHUTTLE
Is that a fact?

WOODLY
The maid just quit. The place is a mess. You can start in the master bedroom.

PENELOPE
Please—

SHUTTLE
He's not anybody to tell somebody else what to do in a master bedroom.

PENELOPE
I'll get ready, Herb. I didn't expect you this soon.

   [*To all*]

Please—won't everybody be nice to everybody else while I'm gone?

   [*All freeze, except for* PENELOPE, *who comes forward to address the audience. Lights on set fade as spotlight comes on*]

Most men shunned me—even when I nearly swooned for want of love. I might as well have been girdled in a chastity belt. My chastity belt was not made of iron and chains and chickenwire, but of Harold's lethal reputation.

   [SHUTTLE *comes into the spotlight*]

SHUTTLE
I keep having this nightmare—that he catches us.

PENELOPE
Doing what?

SHUTTLE
He'd kill me. He'd be right to kill me, too—the kind of guy he is.

PENELOPE
Or was. We haven't done anything wrong, you know.

SHUTTLE
He'd assume we had.

PENELOPE
That's something, I suppose.

SHUTTLE
All through the day I'm so confident. That's why I'm such a good salesman, you know? I have confidence, and I look like I have confidence, and that gives other people confidence. People laugh sometimes when they find out I'm a vacuum cleaner salesman. They stop laughing, though, when they find out I made forty-three thousand dollars last year. I've got six other salesmen working under me, and what they all plug into is *my* confidence. That's what charges them up.

PENELOPE
I'm glad.

SHUTTLE
I was captain of the wrestling team at Lehigh University.

PENELOPE
I know.

SHUTTLE
If you want to wrestle, you go to Lehigh. If you want to play tennis, you go to Vanderbilt.

PENELOPE
I don't want to go to Vanderbilt.

SHUTTLE
You don't wrestle if you don't have supreme confidence, and I wrestled. But when I get with you, and I say to myself, "My God—here I am with the wife of Harold Ryan, one of the great heroes of all time-—"

  [*Pause*]

PENELOPE
Yes?

SHUTTLE
Something happens to my confidence.

PENELOPE

  [*To the audience*]

This conversation took place, incidentally, about three months before Harold was declared legally dead.

SHUTTLE
When Harold is definitely out of the picture, Penelope,

when I don't have to worry about doing him wrong or you wrong or Paul wrong, I'm going to ask you to be my wife.

PENELOPE
I'm touched.

SHUTTLE
That's when I'll get my confidence back.

PENELOPE
I see.

SHUTTLE
If you'll pardon the expression, that's when you'll see the fur and feathers fly. Good night.

PENELOPE
Good night.

[*Blackout*]

SCENE TWO

SHUTTLE and WOODLY argue in pitch
darkness, with PAUL listening, and
lights come up gradually to full on the
living room the same evening.

SHUTTLE
You've got to fight from time to time.

WOODLY
Not true.

SHUTTLE
Or get eaten alive.

WOODLY
That's not true either—or needn't be, unless we make it
true.

SHUTTLE
Phooey.

WOODLY
Which we do. But we can stop doing that.

> [*The lights are full.* SHUTTLE *and* WOODLY *are bored
> with each other.* WOODLY *looks out the window, speaks*

to an imaginary listener who has more brains than SHUTTLE. PAUL *hates them both, but prefers* SHUTTLE's *noisy manliness*]

We simply stop doing that—dropping things on each other, eating each other alive.

SHUTTLE

[*Calling*]

Penelope! We're late!

PENELOPE

[*Off, in master bedroom suite*]

Coming.

SHUTTLE

[*To* PAUL]

Women are always late. You'll find out.

WOODLY

[*Thoughtfully*]

The late Mrs. Harold Ryan.

SHUTTLE
I'm sick of this argument. I just have one more thing to say: If you elect a President, you support him, no matter

what he does. That's the only way you can have a
country!

WOODLY
It's the planet that's in ghastly trouble now and all our
brothers and sisters thereon.

SHUTTLE
None of my relatives are Chinese Communists. Speak for
yourself.

WOODLY
Chinese maniacs and Russian maniacs and American
maniacs and French maniacs and British maniacs have
turned this lovely, moist, nourishing blue-green ball into a
doomsday device. Let a radar set and a computer mistake
a hawk or a meteor for a missile, and that's the end of
mankind.

SHUTTLE
You can believe that if you want. I talk to guys like you,
and I want to commit suicide.

[*To* PAUL]

You get that weight-lifting set I sent you?

PAUL
It came yesterday. I haven't opened it yet.

WOODLY

[*Musingly, attempting to find the idea acceptable, even
funny, in a way*]

Maybe it's supposed to end now. Maybe God wouldn't have it any other way.

SHUTTLE

[*To* PAUL]

Start with the smallest weights. Every week add a pound or two.

WOODLY
Maybe God has let everybody who ever lived be reborn—so he or she can see how it ends. Even Pithecanthropus erectus and Australopithecus and Sinanthropus pekensis and the Neanderthalers are back on Earth—to see how it ends. They're all on Times Square—making change for peepshows. Or recruiting Marines.

SHUTTLE

[*To* PAUL]

You ever hear the story about the boy who carried a calf around the barn every day?

WOODLY
He died of a massive rupture.

SHUTTLE
You think you're so funny. You're not even funny.

[*To* PAUL]

Right? Right? You don't hurt yourself if you start out slow.

WOODLY
You're preparing him for a career in the slaughterhouses of
Dubuque?

[*To* PAUL]

Take care of your body, yes! But don't become a
bender of horseshoes and railroad spikes. Don't become
obsessed by your musculature. Any one of these poor,
dead animals here was a thousand times the athlete
you can ever hope to be. Their magic was in their
muscles. Your magic is in your brains!

[PENELOPE *enters from the bedroom, dressed for the
fight. She wears barbaric jewelry* HAROLD *gave her years
ago, a jaguar-skin coat over her shoulders*]

PENELOPE

[*Brightly*]

Gentlemen! Is this right for a fight? It's been so long.

SHUTTLE
Beautiful! I've never seen that coat.

PENELOPE
Seven jaguars' skins, I'm told. Harold shot every one. Shall
we go?

WOODLY

[*Sick about the slain jaguars*]

Oh no! Wear a coat of cotton—wear a coat of wool.

PENELOPE
What?

WOODLY
Wear a coat of domestic mink. For the love of God,
though, Penelope, don't lightheartedly advertise that the
last of the jaguars died for you.

SHUTTLE
She's my date tonight. What do you want her to do—
bring the poor old jaguars back to life with a bicycle
pump? Bugger off! Ask Paul what *he* thinks.

   [*To* PAUL]

Your mother looks beautiful—right?

   [PAUL *pointedly declines to answer*]

Kid?

   [PAUL *walks away from him*]

Doesn't your mother look nice?

   [*He goes to* PAUL, *wondering what is wrong*]

Paul?

PAUL

   [*Smolderingly*]

I don't care what she wears.

SHUTTLE
Something's made you sore.

PAUL
Don't worry about it.

SHUTTLE
You bet I'll worry about it. I said something wrong?

PAUL

[*Close to angry tears*]

It's my father's birthday—that's all.

[*Facing everybody, raising his voice*]

That's all. Who cares about that?

SHUTTLE

[*Horrified, raising his hand to swear an oath*]

I had not the slightest inkling.

[*To* PENELOPE, *feeling betrayed*]

Why didn't you say so?

PAUL

[*Bitterly*]

She doesn't care! She's not married any more! She's going to have fun!

[*To* PENELOPE]

I hope you have so much fun you can hardly stand it.

[*To* WOODLY]

Dr. Woodly—I hope you make up even better jokes about my father than the ones you've said so far.

SHUTTLE

[*Reaching out for* PAUL]

Kid—kid—

PAUL

[*To* SHUTTLE]

And I wish you'd quit touching me all the time. It drives me nuts!

SHUTTLE

[*Reaching out again*]

What's this?

PAUL

[*Recoiling*]

Don't!

SHUTTLE

[*Aghast*]

You sure misunderstood something—and we'd better get it straight.

PAUL

Explain it to them. I'm bugging out of here.

[*He grabs a jacket from a chair.* SHUTTLE *is in his way*]

Don't touch me. Get out of the way.

SHUTTLE

Men can touch other men, and it doesn't mean a thing. Haven't you ever seen football players after they've won the Superbowl?

PENELOPE

[*To* PAUL]

Where will you be?

PAUL

Anywhere but here. I'd just sit here and cry about the way my father's been forgotten.

SHUTTLE

I *worship* your father. That stuffed alligator your mother gave me—the one he shot? It's the proudest thing in my apartment.

PAUL

[*At the door*]

Everybody talks about how rotten kids act. Grownups can be pretty rotten, too.

[*He exits through front door, slams it*]

SHUTTLE

[*Heartbroken*]

Kid—kid—

WOODLY

It's good. Let him go.

SHUTTLE

If he'd just come out for the Little League, the way I asked him, he'd find out we touch all the time—shove each other, slug each other, and just horse around.
I'm going to go get him—

WOODLY

Don't! Let him have all the privacy he wants. Let him grieve, let him rage. There has never been a funeral for his father.

PENELOPE
I never knew when to hold it—or who to ask, or what to
say.

WOODLY
Tonight's the night.

SHUTTLE
If he'd just get into scouting, and camp out some, and see
how everybody roughhouses around the fire—

WOODLY
What a beautiful demonstration this is of the utter
necessity of rites of passage.

SHUTTLE
I feel like I've been double-crossed.

[*To* PENELOPE, *peevishly*]

If you'd just told me it was Harold's birthday—

PENELOPE
What then?

SHUTTLE
We could have had some kind of birthday party for him.
We could have taken Paul to the fight with us.

WOODLY
Minors aren't allowed at fights.

SHUTTLE
Then we'd stay home and eat venison or something, and
look through the scrapbooks. I've got a friend who has
a whole freezer full of striped bass and caribou meat.

[*Going to the front door*]

I'm going to bring that boy back.

[*He exits through front door*]

WOODLY

[*Going to* PENELOPE]

This is very good for us.

PENELOPE
It is?

WOODLY
The wilder Paul is tonight, the calmer he'll be tomorrow.

PENELOPE
As long as he keeps out of the park.

WOODLY
After this explosion, I think, he'll be able to accept the fact
that his mother is going to marry again.

PENELOPE
The only thing I ever told him about life was, "Keep out of
the park after the sun goes down."

WOODLY
We've got to dump Shuttle.

[*Pointing to the vacuum cleaner*]

He brings his vacuum cleaner on *dates?*

PENELOPE
That's the XKE.

WOODLY
The what?

PENELOPE
It's an experimental model. He doesn't dare leave it
in his car, for fear it will fall into the hands of
competition.

WOODLY
What kind of a life is that?

PENELOPE
He told me one time what the proudest moment of his life
was. He made Eagle Scout when he was twenty-nine
years old.

[*Clinging to him suddenly*]

Oh, Norbert—promise me that Paul has not gone into the
park!

WOODLY

[*Pause*]

If you warned him against it as much as you say, it's almost a certainty.

PENELOPE

[*Petrified*]

No! Oh no! Three people murdered in there in the last six weeks! The police won't even go in there any more.

WOODLY
I wish Paul luck.

PENELOPE
It's suicide!

WOODLY
I'd be dead by now if that were the case.

PENELOPE
Meaning?

WOODLY
Every night, Penelope, for the past two years, I've made it a point to walk through the park at midnight.

PENELOPE
Why would you do that?

WOODLY
To show myself how brave I am. The issue's in doubt, you know—since I'm always for peace—

PENELOPE
I'm amazed.

WOODLY
Me, too. I know something not even the police know—
what's in the park at midnight. Nothing. Or, when I'm
in there, there's me in there. Fear and nobody and me.

PENELOPE
And maybe Paul. What about the murderers? They're in
there!

WOODLY
They didn't murder me.

PENELOPE
Paul's only twelve years old.

WOODLY
He can make the sound of human footsteps—which is a
terrifying sound.

PENELOPE
We've got to rescue him.

WOODLY
If he is in the park, luck is all that can save him now, and
there's plenty of that.

PENELOPE
He's not your son.

WOODLY
No. But he's going to be. If he is in the park and he
comes out safely on the other side, I can say to him, "You
and I are the only men with balls enough to walk
through the park at midnight."

[*Pause*]

On that we can build.

PENELOPE
It's a jungle out there.

WOODLY
That's been said before.

PENELOPE
He'd go to a movie. I think that's what he'd do. If I were
sure he was in a movie, I could stop worrying. We
could have him paged.

[*Lion doorbell roars*]

WOODLY
I hate that thing.

[*He opens door, admits* SHUTTLE, *who carries a bakery
box*]

PENELOPE
Did you see him?

SHUTTLE
Yeah.

PENELOPE
Is he all right?

SHUTTLE
Far as I know.

PENELOPE
Is he coming home?

SHUTTLE
He ditched me. He started running, and I started running, then he lost me in the park.

PENELOPE
The park!

SHUTTLE
It's dark in there.

PENELOPE
And that's where he is!

SHUTTLE
I figure he ducked in one place and ducked out another.

PENELOPE

[*Disgusted with him*]

You figure!

SHUTTLE
Then I saw this bakery store that was still open, so I
bought a birthday cake.

PENELOPE
A what?

SHUTTLE
For Harold. When Paul comes home, we can have some
birthday cake.

PENELOPE
How nice.

SHUTTLE
They had this cake somebody else hadn't picked up. It
says, "Happy Birthday, Somebody Else."

WOODLY
"Happy Birthday, Wanda June!"

SHUTTLE
We can take off the "Wanda June" with a butter knife.

PENELOPE
Did you talk to Paul?

SHUTTLE
Before he started to run. He said his father carried a key
to this apartment around his neck—and someday we'd
all hear the sound of that key in the door.

PENELOPE
We've got to find him.

[*Preparing to exit through front door*]

I want you to show me exactly where you saw him last.

[*To* WOODLY]

And you stay here, Norbert, in case he comes home.

[*To* SHUTTLE]

That's all he said—the thing about the key?

SHUTTLE
He said one other thing. It wasn't very nice.

PENELOPE
What was it?

SHUTTLE
He told me to take a flying fuck at the moon.

[*Blackout*]

SCENE THREE

DARKNESS.   Lights come up on living room. WOODLY is alone, asleep on the couch.

HAROLD lets himself and LOOSELEAF in through the front door—quietly. HAROLD has a full beard and a paunch. LOOSELEAF is skinnier. He has a handlebar moustache. Both wear new sports clothes and smoke expensive cigars. HAROLD is calm. LOOSELEAF is nervous, confused. They prowl the room cautiously, checking this and that. HAROLD awakens WOODLY by playing with his feet.

WOODLY

[*Startled*]

Ooops.

HAROLD

[*To* LOOSELEAF, *very amused*]

Ooops.

WOODLY
Can I—uh—help you gentlemen?

HAROLD

[*Moving downstage, feeling at home*]

Gentlemen—that's nice.

WOODLY

[*To* LOOSELEAF]

You startled me.

LOOSELEAF
Yeah. We just got here.

WOODLY
I thought you might be burglars—but you're not, I hope.

LOOSELEAF
Nope.

[*Idiotically, incapable of deception*]

I got a lot of stuff.

WOODLY

[*Looking at him closely*]

You do?

HAROLD
The door was unlocked. Is it always unlocked?

WOODLY
It's always *locked*.

HAROLD
But here *you* are inside, aren't you?

WOODLY
You're—you're old friends of Harold Ryan?

HAROLD
We tried to be. We tried to be.

WOODLY
He's dead, you know.

HAROLD
Dead! Such a *final* word. Dead!

   [*To* LOOSELEAF]

Did you hear that?

LOOSELEAF
Yup.

   [*Telephone rings.* WOODLY *answers, keeping his eyes on the bizarre guests*]

WOODLY
Hello? Oh—hello, Mother.

HAROLD

[*To* LOOSELEAF]

Hello, Mother.

WOODLY
. . . Who? . . . Did she say how far apart the pains
were? . . . When was that? . . . Oh dear.

HAROLD
Oh dear.

WOODLY
Call her back—tell her to head for the hospital. Tell the
hospital to expect her. I'll leave right now.

[*He hangs up, faces the intruders*]

Look—I'm sorry—I have to go.

HAROLD
We'll miss you so.

WOODLY
Look—this isn't my apartment, and there isn't anybody
else here. Mrs. Ryan won't be home for a while.

HAROLD
Oh, oh, oh—I thought it *was* your apartment. You seemed
so at home here.

WOODLY
I'm a neighbor. I have the apartment across the hall. I have to go to the hospital now. An *emergency.*

[HAROLD *is unstirred*]

I mean—I can't leave you here. You'll have to go. I'll tell Mrs. Ryan you were here. You can come back later.

HAROLD
Ahh—then she's still alive.

WOODLY
She's fine. Please—

HAROLD
And still Mrs. Harold Ryan?

WOODLY
Will you please go? An emergency!

HAROLD
She still has just the one child—the boy?

[*He moves slowly toward the front door, with* WOODLY *trying to hustle him and* LOOSELEAF *out*]

WOODLY
Yes! Yes! The boy! One boy!

HAROLD

[*Stopping*]

And what, exactly, is your relationship to Mrs. Ryan?

WOODLY
Neighbor! Doctor! I live across the hall.

HAROLD
And you come into Mrs. Ryan's apartment as often as you please, looking into various health matters?

WOODLY
Yes! Please! You've got to get out right now!

[HAROLD *moves a little more, stops again*]

HAROLD
Just her neighbor and doctor? That's all?

WOODLY

[*At the end of his patience, blurting*]

And her fiancé!

HAROLD

[*Delighted*]

And her fiancé! How nice. I hope you'll be very happy— or is that what one says to the woman?

WOODLY
I've got to run!

[*He turns out the overhead light*]

HAROLD
You wish the woman good luck, and you tell the man how
fortunate he is. That's how it goes.

WOODLY

[*Holding open the front door*]

I've literally got to run!

HAROLD
I won't try to keep up with you. I'm not as fast on my feet
as I once was.

[*All three exit. A moment later,* HAROLD *lets himself
and* LOOSELEAF *in again with a key. He turns on the
light again, roams the room, reacquainting himself with
his beloved trophies.* LOOSELEAF *is jangled by the
adventure.* HAROLD *chucks a lioness under her chin*]

Miss me, baby?

LOOSELEAF
I dunno, boy.

HAROLD
Hm?

LOOSELEAF
It's a bitch.

HAROLD

[*Quietly*]

A bitch.

LOOSELEAF
Didn't recognize you.

HAROLD
We've never met.

LOOSELEAF
I wonder who'll recognize us first? They'll wet their pants.

HAROLD
I hope the men do. I would rather the women didn't.

LOOSELEAF
I'm gonna wet *my* pants.

[*He laughs idiotically*]

HAROLD

[*Looking around himself*]

Home, sweet home.

LOOSELEAF
One thing, anyway—at least Penelope didn't throw out all
your crap. I bet Alice threw out all my crap after I'd
been gone a week.

HAROLD
We'll see.

[HAROLD, *who wants to savor the early moments of his homecoming alone, now tries to get the very jumpy* LOOSELEAF *out of the apartment*]

It appears that we're going to have to wait awhile for any more action here, Colonel. Why don't you run on home while the evening's young.

LOOSELEAF
Home. Jesus.

[*He makes his hands tremble*]

I'm like *this*. Home!

HAROLD
Home is important to a man.

LOOSELEAF
You know what gets me?

HAROLD

[*Absently*]

No.

LOOSELEAF
How all the magazines show tits today.

HAROLD
Um.

LOOSELEAF
Used to be against the law, didn't it?

HAROLD

[*Fed up with* LOOSELEAF]

I suppose.

LOOSELEAF

[*Making no move to leave*]

Must have changed that law.

[*Silence, while* HAROLD *attempts to be alone, even though* LOOSELEAF *is still present*]

HAROLD

[*Thoughtfully hefting a broadsword, admiring its balance and strength*]

Home.

LOOSELEAF
You know what gets me?

[HAROLD *does not respond*]

You know what gets me?

HAROLD

[*To himself*]

Oh, shit.

LOOSELEAF

[*Finding enough encouragement in this*]

How everybody says "fuck" and "shit" all the time. I used to be scared shitless I'd say "fuck" or "shit" in public, by accident. Now everybody says "fuck" and "shit," "fuck" and "shit" all the time. Something very big must have happened while we were out of the country.

HAROLD

[*Flatly*]

Looseleaf—will you get the hell home?

LOOSELEAF
At least we found the diamonds.

HAROLD
At least!

LOOSELEAF
I'd really feel stupid if we didn't bring anything back home.

HAROLD
It's enough that you've brought yourself home!

LOOSELEAF
I wish you'd tell Alice that. And that Goddamn Mrs.
Wheeler.

HAROLD

[*Hotly*]

Tell them yourself!

LOOSELEAF
You don't know my mother-in-law, boy.

HAROLD
After eight years in the jungle with you, I know Mrs.
Wheeler better than I know anybody in the universe!

LOOSELEAF
I didn't tell you everything.

HAROLD
The time we were in a tree for fourteen days, you certainly
tried to tell me everything about Mrs. Wheeler.

LOOSELEAF
I didn't even scratch the surface. You're lucky, boy. You
come home, and nobody's here. When I go home,
everybody's going to be there.

HAROLD
This room is full of ghosts.

LOOSELEAF
You're lucky, boy. My house is gonna be filled with *people*.

[HAROLD *ignores this, attempts to savor the ghosts in the room*]

You know what gets me?

HAROLD
Go home!

LOOSELEAF
Thank God we found the fucking diamonds!

HAROLD
The hell with the diamonds!

LOOSELEAF
You were rich *before*. This is the first time I was ever rich.

HAROLD
Go home! Show them how rich you are for a change!

LOOSELEAF
Can I have the Cadillac?

HAROLD
Take the Cadillac and drive it off a cliff, for all I care.

LOOSELEAF
What'll you do for transportation?

HAROLD
I'll buy a hundred more Cadillacs. Go home!

LOOSELEAF
You know what gets me about that Cadillac?

HAROLD
Go home!

LOOSELEAF
When I drive it, I feel like I'm in the middle of a great big wad of bubblegum. I don't hear anything, I don't feel anything. I figure somebody else is driving. It's a bitch.

HAROLD
Go home.

LOOSELEAF
I'm liable to find anything!

HAROLD
That's the point! Walk in there and find whatever there *is* to find—before Alice can cover it up.

LOOSELEAF
I know, I know. I dunno. At least she's in the same house. Sure was spooky, looking in the window there, and there she was.

HAROLD
So long, Colonel.

LOOSELEAF
You know what gets me?

HAROLD

[*Taking hold of* LOOSELEAF *and steering him to the front door*]

Let's talk about it some other time.

LOOSELEAF
How short the skirts are.

HAROLD

[*Opening the door*]

Good night, Colonel. It's been beautiful.

LOOSELEAF
Something very important about sex must have happened while we were gone.

[HAROLD *shoves him out of the apartment and shuts the door.* HAROLD *starts to roam the room again, but the lion doorbell roars*]

HAROLD

[*Going to the door*]

Hell!

[HAROLD *opens the door.* LOOSELEAF *comes in*]

LOOSELEAF
You know what gets me? Those guys who went to the
moon! To the *moon,* boy!

HAROLD
Leave me alone! After eight years of horrendously close
association, the time has come to part! I crave solitude
and time for reflection—and then a reunion in privacy
with my own flesh and blood. You and I may not
meet again for months!

LOOSELEAF
Months?

HAROLD
I'm certainly not going to come horning back into
your life tomorrow, and I will not welcome your horning
back into mine. A chapter has ended. We are old
comrades—at a parting of the ways.

LOOSELEAF

   [*Bleakly, shrugging*]

I'm lonesome already.

   [*He exits*]

HAROLD

   [*Roaming the room again*]

The moon. The new heroism—put a village idiot into a pressure cooker, seal it up tight, and shoot him at the moon.

[*To his portrait*]

Hello there, young man. In case you're wondering, I could beat the shit out of you. And any woman choosing between us—sorry, kid, she'd choose me.

[*Pleased with the room*]

I must say, this room is very much as I left it.

[*He sees the cake*]

What's this? A cake? "Happy Birthday, Wanda June"? Who the hell is Wanda June?

[*Blackout*]

SCENE FOUR

MUSIC indicates happiness, innocence,
and weightlessness. Spotlight comes
up on WANDA JUNE, a lisping
eight-year-old in a starched party
dress. She is as cute as Shirley
Temple.

WANDA JUNE
Hello. I am Wanda June. Today was going to be my
birthday, but I was hit by an ice-cream truck before I could
have my party. I am dead now. I am in Heaven. That is
why my parents did not pick up the cake at the bakery.
I am not mad at the ice-cream truck driver, even though
he was drunk when he hit me. It didn't hurt much. It
wasn't even as bad as the sting of a bumblebee. I am really
happy here! It's so much fun. I am glad the driver was
drunk. If he hadn't been, I might not have got to Heaven
for years and years and years. I would have had to go
to high school first, and then beauty college. I would have
had to get married and have babies and everything.
Now I can just play and play and play. Any time I want
any pink cotton candy I can have some. Everybody
up here is happy—the animals and the dead soldiers and
people who went to the electric chair and everything.
They're all glad for whatever sent them here. Nobody is

mad. We're all too busy playing shuffleboard. So if
you think of killing somebody, don't worry about it. Just
go ahead and do it. Whoever you do it to should kiss
you for doing it. The soldiers up here just love the shrapnel
and the tanks and the bayonets and the dum dums that
let them play shuffleboard all the time—and drink beer.

[*Spotlight begins to dim and carnival music on a steam
calliope begins to intrude, until, at the end of the speech,*
WANDA JUNE *is drowned out and the stage is black*]

We have merry-go-rounds that don't cost anything to ride
on. We have Ferris wheels. We have Little League and
girls' basketball. There's a drum and bugle corps anybody
can join. For people who like golf, there is a par-three
golf course and a driving range, with never any waiting.
If you just want to sit and loaf, why that's all right, too.
Gourmet specialties are cooked to your order and served
at any time of night or day. . . .

[*Sudden silence*]

WOODY WOODPECKER VOICE
Ha ha ha *ha* ha!

[*Pistol shot*]

You got me, pal.

[*Silence*
Spotlight comes up on LOOSELEAF HARPER, *who wears
the clothes he will wear in the next scene—new sports*

*clothes, a shirt open at the neck. As always, he is
friendly and embarrassed*]

LOOSELEAF
When Penelope asked me to say something about dropping
the bomb on Nagasaki, I didn't give a very good answer,
I guess. It's a very complicated question. Jesus—you
know? You have to explain what it's like to be in the Air
Force and how they give you your orders and all that.
What it feels like to be in a plane, what the world looks like
down there. After I got home from the war, the minister
of my church asked me if I would speak to a scout troop
that met in the church basement. So I did. They met
on Thursday nights. I used to belong to that troop. I never
made Eagle Scout. But you know something? It's a very
strange kind of kid that makes Eagle Scout. They
always seem so lonesome, like they'd worked real hard to
get a job nobody else cares about. They get a whole
bunch of merit badges. That's how you get to be an Eagle
Scout. I don't think I had over five or six merit badges. The
only one I remember is Public Health.
That was a bitch. The Boy Scout Manual said I was
supposed to find out what my town did about sewage.
Jesus, they just dumped it all in Sugar Creek.

[*He laughs idiotically*]

Sugar Creek! That was a long time ago, but it's all
coming back to me now. There was another merit badge
you could get for roller skating. There used to be a
roller rink at a bend in Sugar Creek, up above where the
sewage went in. I got in a fight there one time. I had

on roller skates, and the guy I was fighting had
on basketball shoes. He had a tremendous advantage
over me. He was a little guy, but he beat the shit out of
me. I had to laugh like hell. Don't ever fight a guy when
you've got on roller skates.

[*Silence*]

Jesus—I remember my mother used to make me chew
bananas for a full minute before I swallowed—so I
wouldn't get sick. Makes you wonder what else your
parents told you that wasn't *true*.

[*Blackout*]

SCENE FIVE

SPOTLIGHT comes up on HAROLD. He
sits on the front seat of an imaginary
car. The seat is covered with zebra
skin.

HAROLD
The night I met Penelope, I had no beard—so imagine
me, if you can, without a beard. Actually, I wasn't as
good-looking then as I am now. And, if anything, my
health has improved. At any rate—I had just come home
from Kenya—to discover that my third wife, Mildred,
like the two before her, had become a drunken bum.
In my experience, alcoholism is far more prevalent
among women than men. So I got into my automobile—

[He pantomimes turning the ignition key. The sound of
a starter and a powerful engine responds. He
pantomimes putting the car in gear and driving away
from the curb. Appropriate sounds are heard]

I drove through the night, until I was attracted by a
sign which said—

[Spotlight comes up on PENELOPE, who wears a
skimpy carhop outfit she has had on under her coat in
the previous scene]

"Hamburger Heaven."

PENELOPE
Heaven.

[HAROLD *pantomimes swerving into Hamburger
Heaven. Tires squeal. He pantomimes a stop, kills the
engine. He blows his imaginary horn. A real horn
blows the bugle call for "charge."* PENELOPE *crosses to*
HAROLD]

Can I help you, sir?

HAROLD
I think so, daughter. How old are you?

PENELOPE
Eighteen—

[*Pause*]

and a half.

HAROLD
A springbok, an oryx, a gemsbok—a gazelle.

PENELOPE
Sir?

HAROLD
Raw hamburger, please—and a whole onion. I want to eat
the onion like an apple. Do you understand?

PENELOPE
Yes, sir.

[*To the audience*]

It was a very unusual automobile. It was a Cadillac, but it had water buffalo horns where the bumpers should be.

[*To* HAROLD]

And what to drink?

HAROLD
What time do you get off work, my child?

PENELOPE
I'm sorry, sir, I'm engaged to be married. My boyfriend would be mad if I went out with another man.

HAROLD
Did you ever daydream that you would one day meet a friendly millionaire?

PENELOPE
I'm engaged.

HAROLD
Daughter—I love you very much.

PENELOPE
You don't even *know* me.

HAROLD
You are woman. I know woman well.

PENELOPE
This is crazy.

HAROLD
Destiny often seems that way. You're going to marry me.

PENELOPE
What do you do for a living?

HAROLD
My parents died in an automobile accident when I was
sixteen years old. They left me a brewery and a baseball
team—and other things. I *live* for a living. I've just come
back from Kenya—in Africa. I've been hunting Mau
Mau there.

PENELOPE
Some kind of animal?

HAROLD
The pelt is black. It's a kind of man.

   [*Blackout*]

SCENE SIX

CURTAIN rises on empty living room.
PAUL lets himself in with a key.

PAUL
Mom?

[*Silence*]

Herb?

[*Silence*]

Dr. Woodly?

[*He advances into room uneasily*]

Hello?

[*He sees the cake*]

A cake? Who's Wanda June?

[HAROLD *enters quietly from the kitchen, holding a can
of beer*]

Anybody home?

HAROLD
As a matter of fact—

PAUL

   [*Nearly jumping out of his skin*]

Sir?

HAROLD
As a matter of fact—*I* am home.

PAUL

   [*Thinking* HAROLD *may be a burglar*]

Hello.

HAROLD

   [*Simply*]

Hello.

PAUL
Are you—

   [*His voice fails him*]

HAROLD

   [*Hoping to be recognized*]

You were about to ask a question?

PAUL
Are you—do you—

HAROLD
Ask it!

PAUL

[*Blurting*]

Do you know who Wanda June is?

HAROLD
Life has denied me that thrill.

PAUL
Do you mind if I ask who you are?

HAROLD
Mind?

[*Aside*]

God, yes, I mind.

[*To* PAUL]

I'm your father's friend. A man claiming to be the family physician let me in a while ago.

PAUL
Dr. Woodly.

HAROLD
Dr. Woodly. I should make a little list.

PAUL
Is anybody besides you here now?

HAROLD
The doctor was called away on an emergency. I think it was birth.

PAUL
Where's Mom?

HAROLD
You don't *know* where your mother is? Does she put on a short skirt and go drinking all night?

PAUL
She went to the fight with Herb Shuttle, I guess.

HAROLD
You think you could find me a pencil and paper?

PAUL
I'll see.

   [*He rummages through a drawer*]

HAROLD
And you've been roaming the streets while your mother is God-knows-where?

PAUL
I was going to a funny movie, but I changed my mind. If you're depressed, laughing doesn't help much.

[*He gives* HAROLD *pencil and paper*]

When did you know my father?

HAROLD
Man and boy.

PAUL
Everybody says he was so brave.

HAROLD
Even this—"Herb Shuttle," you said?

PAUL
He *worships* Father.

HAROLD

[*Pleased*]

Ah! And what sort of man *is* this worshiper?

PAUL
He's a vacuum cleaner salesman.

HAROLD

[*Deflated*]

I see.

[*Recovering*]

And he came into the apartment one day, to demonstrate his wares, and your mother, as it happened, was charmingly *en deshabille*—

PAUL
She met him at college.

HAROLD

[*Startled*]

College!

PAUL
They were in the same creative writing class.

HAROLD
College?

PAUL
She has a master's degree in English literature.

HAROLD
What a pity! Educating a beautiful woman is like pouring honey into a fine Swiss watch. Everything stops.

[*Pause*]

And the doctor? He worships your father, too?

PAUL
He insults him all the time.

HAROLD

   [*Delighted*]

Excellent!

PAUL
What's good about that?

HAROLD
It makes life spicy.

PAUL
He doesn't do it in front of me, but he does it with Mother.

   [*Indicating* HAROLD'*s portrait*]

You know what he called Father one time?

HAROLD
No.

PAUL
"Harold, the Patron Saint of Taxidermy."

HAROLD

   [*Measuring his opponent*]

What does he do—of an athletic nature?

PAUL
Nothing. He plays a violin in a doctors' quartet.

HAROLD
Aha! He has a brilliant military record, I'm sure.

PAUL
He was a stretcher-bearer in the Korean War.

[*Pause*]

Were you in a war with Father?

HAROLD
Big ones, little ones, teeny-weeny ones—just and otherwise.

PAUL
Tell me some true stories about Dad.

HAROLD

[*Unused to the word*]

"Dad?"

[*Accepting it*]

Dad.

[*To himself*]

The boy wants tales of derring-do. Name a country.

PAUL
England?

HAROLD

[*Disgusted*]

Oh hell.

PAUL
Dad was never in England?

HAROLD
Behind a desk for a little while.

[*Contemptuously*]

A desk! They had him planning air raids. A city can't
flee like a coward or fight like a man, and the choice
between fleeing and fighting was at the core of the life of
Harold Ryan. There was only one thing he enjoyed
more than watching someone make that choice,
and that was making the choice himself. Ask about
Spain, where he was the youngest soldier in the
Abraham Lincoln Brigade. He was a famous sniper.
They called him
"La Picadura"—"the sting."

PAUL

[*Echoing wonderingly*]

"The sting."

HAROLD
As in "Death, where is thy sting?" He killed at least
fifty men, wounded hundreds more.

PAUL

[*Slightly dismayed at such murderousness*]

"The sting."

HAROLD
Ask about the time he and I were parachuted into
Yugoslavia to join a guerrilla band—in the war against
the Nazis.

PAUL
Tell me that.

HAROLD
I saw your father fight Major Siegfried von Konigswald,
the Beast of Yugoslavia, hand to hand.

PAUL

[*His excitement rising*]

Tell me that! Tell me that!

HAROLD
Hid by day—fought by night. At sunset one day, your
father and I, peering through field glasses, saw a black
Mercedes draw up to a village inn. It was escorted by
two motorcyclists and an armored car. Out of the Mercedes
stepped one of the most hateful men in all of history
—the Beast of Yugoslavia.

PAUL
Wow.

HAROLD
We blacked our hands and faces. At midnight we crept out of the forest and into the village. The name of the village was Mhravitch. Remember that name!

PAUL
Mhravitch.

HAROLD
We came up behind a sentry, and your father slit his throat before he could utter a sound.

PAUL

[*Involuntarily*]

Uck.

HAROLD
Don't care for cold steel? A knife is worse than a bullet?

PAUL
I don't know.

HAROLD
The story gets hairier. Should I stop?

PAUL
Go on.

HAROLD
We caught another Kraut alone in a back lane. Your father choked him to death with a length of piano wire.

Your father was quite a virtuoso with piano wire. That's nicer than a knife, isn't it—as long as you don't look at the face afterwards. The face turns a curious shade of avocado. I must ask the doctor why that is. At any rate, we stole into the back of the inn, and, with the permission of the management, we poisoned the wine of six Krauts who were carousing there.

PAUL
Where did you get the poison?

HAROLD
We carried cyanide capsules. We were supposed to swallow them in case we were captured. It was your father's opinion that the Krauts needed them more than we did at the time.

PAUL
And one of them was the Beast of Yugoslavia?

HAROLD
The Beast was upstairs, and he came running downstairs, for his men were making loud farewells and last wills and testaments—editorializing about the hospitality they had received. And your father said to him in perfect German, which he had learned in the Spanish Civil War, "Major, something tragic seems to have happened to your bodyguard. I am Harold Ryan, of the United States of America. You, I believe, are the Beast of Yugoslavia."

[*Blackout*]

SCENE SEVEN

SILENCE. Pitch blackness. The sounds
of a Nazi rally come up slowly: "Sieg
Heil! Sieg Heil! Sieg Heil!" Spotlight
comes up on MAJOR SIEGFRIED VON
KONIGSWALD, an officer in the dreaded
SS. He is in full ceremonial uniform.
The sounds fade.

VON KONIGSWALD

[*Sadly, resignedly, remembering*]

Ja ja. Ja ja.

[*Pause*]

I am Major Siegfried von Konigswald. They used to call
me "The Beast of Yugoslavia," on account of all the
people I had tortured and shot—and hanged. We'd bop
'em on the head. We'd hook 'em up to the electricity.
We'd stick 'em with hypodermic syringes full of all kinds
of stuff. One time we killed a guy with orange juice. There
was a train wreck, and two of the freight cars were
loaded with oranges, so we had oceans of orange juice.
It was a joke—how much orange juice we had. And we

were interrogating a guy one day, and he wouldn't talk,
and the next thing I know—somebody's filling up this
big syringe with orange juice.

[*Pause*]

There was a guerrilla war going on. You couldn't tell who
was a guerrilla and who wasn't. Even if you got one, it
was still a civilian you got. Telling Americans what a
guerrilla war is like—that's coals to Newcastle. How do
you like that for idiomatic English? "Coals to Newcastle."

[*He laughs*]

That Harold Ryan—he says he spoke to me in perfect
German? He talks German like my ass chews gum. I'm
glad to hear the wonderful thing he said before he killed
me. I sure didn't understand it the first time around. I
figured he was a Lithuanian or something, which will give
you an idea of how wrong you can be. All I knew was he
was very proud about something, and he had a machine
pistol, and it was aimed at me. The woods were full of
all kinds of nuts who were proud of some damn thing
or other, and they all had guns. They were always looking
for revenge. You find a way to bottle revenge—
that's the end of Schnapps *und* Coca-Cola.

[*Pause*]

Harold Ryan said he killed maybe two hundred guys. I
killed a hundred times that many, I bet. That's still
peanuts, of course, compared to what that crazy Looseleaf
did. Harold and me—we was doing it the hard way. I

hope the record books will show that. There should be a
little star or something by the names of the guys
who did it the hard way.

[*Pause*]

I'm up in Heaven now, like that little Wanda June kid. I
wasn't hit by no ice-cream truck. Harold Ryan killed me
with his bare hands. He was good. My eyes popped
out. My tongue stuck out like a red banana. I shit in
my pants. It was a mess.

[*Pause*]

When I got up on the day I died, I said, "What a
beautiful day this is. What a beautiful part of the world."
The whole planet was beautiful. Up here I meet guys
from other planets.

[*He laughs*]

We got some really crazy-looking guys up here. Their
planets weren't anywhere near as nice as Earth. They
had clouds all the time. They never saw a clear blue sky.
They never saw snow. They never saw an ocean.
They had some little lakes, but you couldn't go
swimming in them. The lakes was acid. You go swimming,
you dissolve. We got some guys up here who got
shoved in them lakes. They dissolved.

[*Pause*]

Harold Ryan stopped talking German to me there in

Yugoslavia. He switched to English, so I finally got some kind of idea what he was so burned up about. He wanted revenge for the guy we killed with orange juice. I don't know how he ever found out about it. There was just three of us there when we did it—me and two regular military doctors. Somebody who cleaned up afterwards must have squealed. If I'd lived through the war, and they tried me for war crimes and all that, I'd have to tell the court, I guess, "I was only following orders, as a good soldier should. Hitler *told* me to kill this guy with orange juice."

[*Blackout*]

SCENE EIGHT

DARKNESS. Lights come up on living
room. HAROLD has just finished telling
his true war story to PAUL.

HAROLD
Mhravitch. Remember that name.

PAUL
Mhravitch.

HAROLD
The name will live forever. It was there that Harold Ryan
slew the Beast of Yugoslavia. Mhravitch.

PAUL
When I grow up, I'm going to go to Mhravitch.

HAROLD
It's rather a disappointment these days. It isn't there
any more.

PAUL
Sir?

HAROLD
The Germans shot everybody who lived there, then leveled

it, plowed it, planted turnips and cabbages in the fertile ground. They wished revenge for the slaying of the Beast of Yugoslavia. To their twisted way of thinking, your father had butchered an Eagle Scout.

[*Abruptly*]

Play lots of contact sports?

PAUL
I wanted to go out for football, but Mom was afraid I'd get hurt.

HAROLD
You're *supposed* to get hurt!

PAUL
Dr. Woodly says he's seen hundreds of children permanently injured by football. He says that when there's a war, everybody goes but football players.

HAROLD
Does it bother you to have your mother engaged to a man like that?

PAUL
They're not engaged.

HAROLD
He seems to think they are. He *told* me they were.

PAUL
Oh no, no, no, no, no. It can't be. How embarrassing.

HAROLD

[*Unexpectedly moved*]

You're a very good boy to respond that way.

PAUL
No, no, no, no, no.

HAROLD
I'd like to use the sanitary facilities, if I may.

PAUL
Go ahead.

[*As* HAROLD *exits*]

No, no, no, no.

[PENELOPE *and* SHUTTLE *enter through front door. They are tremendously relieved to see* PAUL]

PENELOPE
Thank God!

SHUTTLE
What a relief!

PENELOPE

[*Going to* PAUL]

My baby's safe!

[PAUL *angrily avoids her touch*]

What's the matter now?

SHUTTLE
We got a birthday cake, kid. Did you see the cake?

PAUL
Are you and Dr. Woodly engaged?

PENELOPE

[*Stunned*]

Who have you been talking to?

PAUL
What difference does that make? Is Dr. Woodly going
to be my father now?

[*Pause*]

PENELOPE
Yes, he is.

PAUL

[*A stifled, gargling cry*]

Aaaaaaaaaaaaaaaaaah!

SHUTTLE

[*Sick*]

That goes double for *me*.

PAUL
I don't want to live any more.

SHUTTLE
I feel like I want to yell my head off—just yell anything.

   [*Yelling*]

Bulllllllllllllllllllllll-dickey!

PAUL
I'll kill myself.

SHUTTLE
The wife of Harold Ryan is going to marry a pansy next?
This is the end of Western Civilization as far as I'm
concerned. You must be crazy as a fruitcake.

PENELOPE
Possibly.

SHUTTLE
How long has this been going on?

PENELOPE
A week. We were waiting for the right time to—

SHUTTLE
I feel as though I had been made a perfect chump of.

PENELOPE
I'm sorry.

SHUTTLE
Marry me instead.

PENELOPE
Thank you, Herb. You're a wonderful man. You really
are. Everybody respects you for what you've done
for scouting and the Little League.

SHUTTLE
You're saying no.

PENELOPE
I'm saying no—and thank you.

SHUTTLE
I didn't make my move fast enough. That's it, isn't it? I
was too respectful.

PENELOPE
You were wonderful.

SHUTTLE
What's so wonderful if I lost the sale?

   [*Turning to* PAUL]

You poor kid.

PAUL
Don't touch me.

SHUTTLE
Wouldn't you rather have your mother marry me than
him?

PAUL
No.

SHUTTLE

[*Moving dazedly toward the front door*]

All my dreams have suddenly collapsed.

[*Pause*]

We did have a lot of laughs together, Penelope.

PENELOPE
It's true.

SHUTTLE
Well—it was nice while it lasted. Thanks for the memories.

[*He exits.
Silence. A toilet flushes loudly and complicatedly*]

PENELOPE
Is Norbert still here?

PAUL
No.

PENELOPE
Then who flushed the toilet?

PAUL
Father's friend.

PENELOPE
What's his name?

PAUL
Don't know.

PENELOPE
For Heaven sakes!

[HAROLD *enters, still adjusting his trousers*]

How do you do?

HAROLD
How do *you* do, Mrs. Ryan? I'd heard you were beautiful,
and so you are. Am I intruding here?

PENELOPE
Not at all.

HAROLD
I couldn't help overhearing that you were about to get
married again.

[PENELOPE *has now recognized him, but attempts to
protect herself from shock by pretending that she has
not*]

PENELOPE
Our family physician has asked me to marry him. Paul
needs the guidance and companionship that only a man
can give. He isn't at all like Harold. But then again, I'm
not the woman I was eight years ago.

[*She slumps into a chair, buries her face in her hands*]

PAUL
Mom?

PENELOPE

[*Pointing weakly*]

That man is your father.

PAUL
What?

PENELOPE
There stand the loins from which you've sprung.

PAUL
I don't get it.

PENELOPE
It *is* you, isn't it, Harold?

HAROLD

[*Enjoying the drama hugely*]

Yes, wife, it is.

[*To* PAUL]

Come here, boy. Your father is home.

PAUL
Sir?

PENELOPE
Go to him.

[PAUL *goes to* HAROLD *dazedly. They embrace clumsily*]

HAROLD	**PAUL**
Son, son, son. . . .	Father, father, father. . . .

[*They part, unsatisfied and confused.* HAROLD *goes to* PENELOPE, *his arms outstretched*]

HAROLD
Wife, wife, wife. . . .

[PENELOPE *struggles to her feet, her face blank.* HAROLD *embraces her, finds himself wrestling with a rigid, unresponsive object*]

Wife, wife, wife. . . .

[HAROLD *lets go, backs away from her*]

What's the matter?

PENELOPE

[*Tearful*]

Give us time.

HAROLD
Like hugging a lamp post.

PENELOPE
Give us time, Harold—to adjust to your being alive.

HAROLD
You were well adjusted to my being dead?

PENELOPE
We adjust to what there is to adjust to. Perhaps Paul, being young, can adjust to joy or grief immediately. I hope he can. I will take a little longer. I'll be as quick as I can.

HAROLD
What sort of time period do you have in mind? Half an hour? An hour?

PENELOPE
I don't know. This is a new disease to me.

HAROLD
Disease?

PENELOPE
Situation.

HAROLD
This reunion isn't what I imagined it would be.

PENELOPE
A telegram—a phone call might have helped.

HAROLD
Seemed the most honest way to begin life together
again—natural, unrehearsed.

PENELOPE
Well—enjoy the natural, honest, unrehearsed
result—surgical shock.

HAROLD
You feel that you're behaving as a woman should?

PENELOPE
Every fuse in my nervous system has been blown.

[*Lion doorbell roars*]

Who's that? Teddy Roosevelt?

[PAUL *answers the door, admits* WOODLY]

WOODLY

[*To* PAUL]

Safe and sound, I see.

[*To* HAROLD]

Oh—you came back.

HAROLD
I came back.

PENELOPE
You *know* each other?

WOODLY
We met here earlier this evening.

PENELOPE
How neat. How keen.

HAROLD
How was the emergency, Doctor? Profitable, I hope.

WOODLY
A policeman delivered the baby in a taxicab.

HAROLD
Tough luck. You'll have to split the fee.

WOODLY

   [*Puzzled by* PENELOPE's *mood*]

Are—are you *crying*, Penelope?

HAROLD
She's crying because she's so happy.

PENELOPE
That's why I'm crying.

PAUL
Dr. Woodly?

   [*Indicating* HAROLD]

You know who this is?

WOODLY
I didn't get his name. A friend of your father?

PAUL
He isn't any friend of Father.

WOODLY
He isn't?

PAUL
He *is* my father.

WOODLY
No!

PENELOPE
Eeeeeeeeeeee-*yup*. Dr. Woodly—I would like you to meet Harold, my husband. Harold, this is Dr. Woodly, my fiancé.

[*She crosses to the door of the master bedroom, kissing each male lightly as she passes*]

Good night, dear. Good night, dear.

[*She stands in the doorway*]

Stay or go, talk or sulk, laugh or cry—as you wish. Do whatever seems called for. My mind is gone. Good night.

[*She exits into bedroom, closes the door firmly, locks it audibly*]

WOODLY

[*Dazedly*]

I feel the same way. What next?

HAROLD
What next? You leave promptly, of course. There is no question as to whose home this is—

WOODLY
None.

HAROLD
Whose son this is, whose wife that is. A fiancé is the most ridiculous appurtenance this household could have at this time. Good night.

WOODLY

[*Crushed, without any possible comeback*]

Good night.

[*He exits through the front door.* HAROLD *goes at once to* PENELOPE's *door, tries it, finds it locked*]

HAROLD
Penelope! God damn it! Penelope!

[*He considers kicking down the door, thinks better of this, turns away*]

Wants to fix up her makeup, no doubt.

PAUL
Is Looseleaf Harper alive?

HAROLD
Alive and hale. He's throwing a little surprise party for his own family. Is your mother often this unstable?

[*Not waiting for an answer, calling again*]

Penelope!

PAUL
She's a real heavy sleeper sometimes.

HAROLD
Why don't you go to bed—son.

PAUL
I can't take my eyes off you.

HAROLD
Tomorrow's another day.

PAUL
You know what my English literature teacher said about you?

HAROLD
Can't it keep till morning?

PAUL
She said you were *legendary*. I wrote a theme about you, and she said, "Your father is a legendary hero out of the Golden Age of Heroes."

HAROLD
That's nice. You thank her for me. Go to bed and get lots of sleep, and then you thank her in the morning.

PAUL
Tomorrow's Saturday. Anyway, she's dead.

HAROLD
Penelope!

PAUL
She was killed in the park two months ago—in the daytime.

HAROLD
Penelope!

PAUL
She was on her way home from a meeting of the African Violet Society, and they got her.

HAROLD

[*Sharply*]

Will you go to bed?

PAUL

[*Stung*]

Yes sir. If you can't wake Mom up, I've got double-decker bunks.

HAROLD

[*Stamping his foot*]

Scat!

[PAUL *exits hastily down the corridor to his room.* HAROLD *goes to* PENELOPE's *door, attempts to woo her through it*]

Penelope—darling—can you hear me? Wife—you know what kept me alive all these fevered, swampy, nightmare years? Your heavenly face, Penelope, my wife —shimmering before me, coaxing me up from my knees, begging me to stagger one step closer to home. Has love ever reached so far? Has love ever overcome more hardships than mine?

[*Silence*]

Has love ever asked more manliness of a man, more womanliness of a woman? Has ever a man done more for a woman's reward?

[*The bedroom door opens, revealing* PENELOPE]

PENELOPE

[*Hollowly, to the world at large*]

There is no one in here of any earthly use to anyone tonight. Tomorrow is another day.

[*She closes the door and locks it*]

HAROLD

[*To audience*]

End of Act One.

[*Blackout*]

ACT TWO

SCENE ONE

DARKNESS. PAUL, alone in the
living room, hammers on his mother's
door. He wears pajamas.

PAUL
Mom! Mother! Mom!

[*Toilet flushes. Lights come up on the living room. It is
morning*]

Dad's got jungle fever, Mom. What'll I do? Mom!

HAROLD

[*A moment of exhaustion*]

Damn.

PAUL
Mom?

[*Door to the master bedroom suite opens.* PENELOPE
*appears in the doorway. She has decided during an
almost sleepless night that she owes it to* PAUL *and to
her own self-respect to explore the possibility of*

beginning her life with HAROLD *anew. She is terrified of him. She hopes that if she can keep calm and open her fears will diminish. Perhaps she can love him again*]

PENELOPE

[*Attempting to behave mechanically as a good wife should*]

What are his symptoms?

PAUL
Shivers and sweats and groans. His teeth chatter. What'll we do?

PENELOPE
What does *he* say to do?

PAUL
He can hardly talk.

HAROLD

[*Responding to a last twinge of nausea*]

Bluh.

PENELOPE
You'd better get Dr. Woodly.

PAUL
Really?

PENELOPE
It *is* an emergency, isn't it?

PAUL

[*Uncertainly*]

Yeah.

PENELOPE
Then get him.

PAUL

[*Thinking she has made a mistake*]

Okay.

[*He exits through front door, leaves door open. We hear him knocking on a door in the hallway*]

Dr. Woodly?

[HAROLD *enters, drained but recovering. He chews on a root. He has slept in the shirt and trousers he wore the night before. He is barefoot.* PAUL *knocks again*]

Dr. Woodly?

[*There is the sound of* WOODLY'*s door opening.* WOODLY *and* PAUL *speak unintelligibly,* WOODLY *evidently inviting* PAUL *in for a moment.* WOODLY'*s door closes*]

HAROLD
What's that all about?

PENELOPE
We thought a doctor might help.

HAROLD
Your old beau?

PENELOPE
We thought it was an emergency.

HAROLD
I don't want that chancre mechanic in here.

PENELOPE
He's a very decent man, Harold.

HAROLD
We all are.

PENELOPE
Shouldn't you lie down?

HAROLD
When I'm dead—

   [*Throwing it away*]

or fucking.

PENELOPE
Paul said you were awfully sick.

HAROLD
I was, I was. It never lasts long.

[*He hears* WOODLY's *door open, is alert to* WOODLY's
approach, continues to speak to PENELOPE *absently*]

The Indians call it "Zamba-keetya"—the little cloudburst.

[WOODLY *and* PAUL *enter.* WOODLY *is correctly
professional and carries a little black bag*]

WOODLY
Ah! You're ambulatory!

HAROLD
What a brilliant diagnosis!

PENELOPE
You know what I want?

[*All look at her*]

I want you both to be friends. I know you both, respect
you both. You *should* be friends.

HAROLD
Nothing would please me more.

PENELOPE

[*Believing him*]

Thank God!

WOODLY

[*Pleased but careful*]

Well now—what seems to be the trouble with the patient today? A touch of malaria, perhaps?

HAROLD
I know malaria. Malaria isn't caused by the bites of bats.

WOODLY
You've been bitten by bats?

HAROLD
Colonel Harper and I once shared a treetop with a family of bats. There was a flash flood. There were piranha fish in the water. That's how Colonel Harper lost his little toe.

WOODLY
You have chills?

HAROLD
Chills, fevers, sweats. You can describe it and name it after yourself: "the Woodly galloping crud."

[WOODLY *enjoys the joke and the blooming friendship*]

You can also describe its cure. I'm eating its cure.

WOODLY
I was going to ask.

HAROLD
Pacqualinincheewa root.

WOODLY
Would you say that again?

HAROLD
Pacqualinincheewa root. Means "cougar fang." Cures anything but a yellow streak down the back.

WOODLY
I've never heard of it.

HAROLD
Congratulations. By crossing twenty-eight feet of cockroach-infested carpet, you've become the third white man ever to hear of it.

WOODLY

[*Fascinated*]

And you've seen it work cures?

HAROLD
Hundreds.

PENELOPE
I'm so glad you like each other. I was so scared, so scared.

HAROLD

[*Breaking off a piece, offering it*]

Have some.

WOODLY
Thank you. Thank you very much.

PENELOPE
I believe in miracles now.

HAROLD
Wasn't that sweet of me?

WOODLY
More and more we find ourselves laying aside false pride
and looking into the pharmacopoeias of primitive people.
Curare, ephedrine—we've found some amazing things.

HAROLD
We have, have we?

WOODLY
That's an editorial *we,* of course. I haven't turned up anything personally.

HAROLD
Everything about you is the editorial *we.* Take that away from you, and you'd disappear.

PENELOPE
Harold!

HAROLD
I could carve a better man out of a banana!

PENELOPE
Please—

HAROLD
You and your damned bedside manner and your damned little black bag full of miracles. You know who filled that bag for you? Not Alice-sit-by-the-fires like yourself. Men with guts filled it, by God—men with guts enough to pay the price for miracles—suffering, ingratitude, loneliness, death—

WOODLY

[*Off balance*]

Good Lord.

HAROLD
I can just hear the editorial wee-wee-weeing when

Looseleaf and I start flying in pacqualinincheewa root.
I can hear the Alice-sit-by-the-fires now: "We discovered
it in the Amazon Rain Forest. Now we cure you with it.
Now we lower our eyes with becoming modesty as we
receive heartfelt thanks."

[HAROLD *suddenly goes to* WOODLY, *takes his hand and
pretends abject gratitude*]

Oh, bless you, Doctor, bless you—oh healer, oh protector,
oh giver of life.

[WOODLY *withdraws his hand, examines it as though it
were diseased*]

PENELOPE
He doesn't *deserve* this! You don't know him. It isn't fair!

HAROLD
He thought he could take my place. It is now my privilege
to give an unambiguous account of why I don't think
he's man enough to do that.

WOODLY
I thought she was a widow.

HAROLD
You were wrong, you quack!

PENELOPE
Awful.

[*Approaching* WOODLY, *but not getting too close*]

I can't tell you how sorry I am.

HAROLD
Say hello to your mother.

PENELOPE

[*Fervently*]

Do say hello to your mother.

WOODLY
I'm taking her to the airport a few minutes from now. She's
going to East St. Louis—to visit an aunt.

PENELOPE
Tell her to have a nice trip.

WOODLY

[*Moving toward the front door*]

Thanks.

[HAROLD *laughs. This stings* WOODLY *to a cold,
peace-loving anger*]

I'm going to have to report you to the Department of
Health.

HAROLD
What for?

WOODLY
Quarantine, possibly. You may be suffering from a loathsome disease which the American people could do without. Goodbye.

[*He exits instantly*]

HAROLD
Now that's what I call fun.

PENELOPE
Ghastly, cruel, unnecessary.

HAROLD
You'll get so you enjoy twitting weaklings again. You used to eat it up.

PENELOPE
I did?

HAROLD
We were one hell of a pair—and we'll be one again. What we need is a honeymoon. Let's start right now.

PENELOPE
A trip, you mean?

HAROLD
I *had* a trip. We'll honeymoon here.

[*To* PAUL]

Go out and play.

PAUL
Play?

HAROLD
Your mother and I do not wish to be disturbed for three full hours.

PENELOPE
He hasn't had breakfast yet.

HAROLD
Buy yourself breakfast.

> [*He takes his billfold from his hip pocket, hands* PAUL *a $100 bill*]

There we go.

PAUL
A hundred dollars!

HAROLD
The smallest thing I've got.

PAUL
Can I get dressed first?

HAROLD
Make it fast.

> [PAUL *exits to his bedroom.* HAROLD *turns to* PENELOPE]

Honeymoon! Honeymoon! Say it: *Honeymoon!*

PENELOPE
It's so—so *stark*.

HAROLD
You used to like it stark!

PENELOPE
Just—*bang*—we have a honeymoon.

HAROLD

[*Beginning to stalk her cunningly*]

I'm not going to strike you. I am going to be as gentle as
pie—as lemon meringue pie. You mustn't run away now.
This is your loving husband approaching. I'm your
husband. Society approves!

[PENELOPE *wants to run, but doesn't*]

Good! You held your ground.

[HAROLD *is very close now, but not touching her*]

Now—turn around, if you would.

PENELOPE
Turn *around?*

HAROLD

[*Laughing*]

I'm not about to introduce to you a jungle novelty. What
I have in mind is massage—a perfectly decent massage.
Turn around, turn around.

[PENELOPE *obeys*]

I'm going to touch your shoulders very gently now. You
mustn't scream.

[*He touches her shoulders gently, expertly*]

So tense, so tense.

PENELOPE
You shouldn't have talked to Norbert that way.

HAROLD
You're thinking with your brain instead of your body.
That's why you're so tense! Forget Norbert. Relax. It's
body time.

PENELOPE
I have a brain.

HAROLD
We all do. But now it's body time. Relax. Ideally, the body
of a woman should feel like a hot water bottle filled with
Devonshire cream. You feel like a paper bag crammed
with curtain rods. Think of your muscles one by one. Let
them go slack. Relax. Let the brain go blank. Relax.
That's the idea—that's my girl. Now the small of the back.
Let those knots over those kidneys unsnarl.

PAUL

[*Entering, dressed to go out and play*]

Dad—

HAROLD

[*Hanging on to* PENELOPE, *but knowing the mood has been broken*]

Couldn't you have vanished quietly out the back door?

PAUL
A hundred dollars for breakfast?

HAROLD
Leave a tip.

PENELOPE

[*Suddenly twisting away, having been nearly hypnotized*]

I have some change.

HAROLD
Ram it up your ass!

[*He realizes at once that his violent side has severely damaged the side of him which is the great seducer.* PENELOPE *and* PAUL *are straight as ramrods*]

I *do* beg your pardon.

[*Sincerely*]

Those words were illy chosen. There is tension in *all* of us
here. Something you must both understand, however, is
that the head of this household is home, and he is
Harold Ryan, and people do what he says when he says it.
That's the way this particular clock is constructed.

[*Lion doorbell roars*]

Sometimes even I hate that thing.

[PAUL *goes reeling to the door in terror, admits*
LOOSELEAF, *who has also been sleeping in his clothes*]

LOOSELEAF

[*Walking right in*]

I've been looking at motorcycles.

HAROLD
Go home!

LOOSELEAF
You ever own a motorcycle?

HAROLD

[*To* PENELOPE]

You're right! We'll take a trip. A trip is what we'll take.

[*To* LOOSELEAF]

I don't want to talk about motorcycles. I don't want to talk about tits. Go home!

LOOSELEAF
Haven't got one.

PENELOPE

[*To* LOOSELEAF]

And you went home unannounced, too?

LOOSELEAF
I dunno. Yeah! Yeah! Yeah! I did.

HAROLD
And how were things?

LOOSELEAF
Let's talk about something else.

PENELOPE

[*To* HAROLD]

Alice got married again.

LOOSELEAF
She *did?*

PENELOPE
You didn't even find *that* out?

LOOSELEAF
There was so much going on.

PENELOPE
She married an accountant named Stanley Kestenbaum.

LOOSELEAF
So that's it! "Kestenbaum, Kestenbaum." Everybody was yelling "Kestenbaum, Kestenbaum." I thought it was some foreign language.

HAROLD
Otherwise, how are things?

LOOSELEAF
I sure didn't expect her to drop dead.

PENELOPE
Dead!

LOOSELEAF
Jesus.

PENELOPE

[*Sick*]

Alice is dead?

LOOSELEAF
No, no—shit no.

[*He stops short*]

Excuse me, Penelope.

PENELOPE
For what?

LOOSELEAF
For saying "shit." Or is that okay now?

PENELOPE

[*Shrilly*]

Who's dead?

LOOSELEAF
My mother-in-law. Fire engines, pulmotors, doctors, cops, coroners—

PENELOPE
What happened?

LOOSELEAF
Well—I walked up to the front door. I was still alive. Big surprise. I rang the doorbell, and old Mrs. Wheeler answered. She had her Goddamn knitting. I said, "Guess who?" She conked right out.

PENELOPE
How horrible.

LOOSELEAF
Yeah—cripes. I never did get any sense out of Alice. She found me holding up the old lady, dead as a

mackerel. It was a bitch. You know—maybe Mrs.
Wheeler was going to die then and there anyway, even if
I'd been the paper boy. Maybe not. I dunno, boy. That's
civilian life for you. Who knows what kills anybody?

HAROLD
Could have happened to anybody.

LOOSELEAF
First Nagasaki—now this.

HAROLD
How about breakfast, wife?

PENELOPE
Breakfast?

HAROLD

[*As though to a waitress*]

Scrambled eggs, kippered herring, fried potatoes—and
a whole onion. I want to eat the onion like an apple. Do
you understand?

[PENELOPE *turns away*]

And lots of orange juice—oceans of orange juice.

PENELOPE
Mrs. Wheeler is dead.

HAROLD
All right—bring me a side order of Mrs. Wheeler.

[*Regarding* LOOSELEAF, *resigning himself to being stuck with his company for a little while longer*]

Oh hell—sit down, Colonel. Penelope will bring you some chow.

PENELOPE
That is the most heartless statement I ever heard pass between human lips.

HAROLD

[*Honestly mystified*]

Which one?

PENELOPE

[*Chokingly*]

"Bring me a side order of Mrs. Wheeler."

HAROLD
She's up in Heaven now. She didn't hear. She is experiencing nothing but pure happiness. There's nothing nicer than that.

[*Suddenly, angrily, slamming a table with his fist*]

Chow! Harold Ryan wants chow!

PENELOPE
What a honeymoon.

HAROLD
Honeymoon temporarily canceled.

[*Catching sight of* PAUL, *whose physical appearance really offends him*]

The boy should still go out and exercise. I have the impression he never gets any exercise. He simply bloats himself with Fig Newtons and bakes his brains over steam radiators.

PENELOPE
You're wrong.

HAROLD
Then let me see him go out and get some exercise.

[*Explosively*]

Right now!

[PAUL *goes reeling in terror to the front door, opens it*]

PAUL

[*To* HAROLD, *abjectly*]

What *kind* of exercise?

HAROLD
Beat the shit out of someone who hates you.

[PAUL *exits.* HAROLD *pounds on a table*]

Chow, chow, chow! God damn it—nutriment!

PENELOPE
We're all going to have to go out for breakfast. The cook
quit yesterday.

HAROLD
You're a woman, aren't you?

[PENELOPE *nods*]

Then we *have* a cook.

[PENELOPE *hesitates*]

Cook, by God! Cook! You're the nigger now.

PENELOPE
People don't use that word any more.

HAROLD
Don't lecture me on race relations. I don't have a molecule
of prejudice. I've been in battle with every kind of man
there is. I've been in bed with every kind of woman
there is—from a Laplander to a Tierra del Fuegian. If I'd
ever been to the South Pole, there'd be a hell of a lot of
penguins who looked like me. Cook!

PENELOPE
You leave me so—so without—without *dignity*.

HAROLD
People now have dignity when frying eggs?

PENELOPE
They don't have to feel like slaves.

HAROLD

[*Grandly*]

Then go now—and fry with dignity—sunnyside up.

[PENELOPE *attempts to respond to this, but is too enraged. She exits, making a tiny mosquito-like hum*]

LOOSELEAF
I dunno, boy.

HAROLD
The educational process.

LOOSELEAF
I guess. You're lucky you don't have any old people around here.

HAROLD
She was about to get married again. She locked me out of the bedroom last night.

[LOOSELEAF *starts to laugh.* HAROLD *shuts him up*]

What's funny about that?

LOOSELEAF

[*Apologetically*]

You know me, boy.

[PENELOPE *enters from the kitchen with a question on her lips*]

HAROLD
I should have torn that door off its hinges. Should have scrogged her ears off. Should have broken the bed.

[*Seeing* PENELOPE]

What do *you* want?

[*Words fail her*]

Well?

PENELOPE
I—I was wondering—is there anything you shouldn't eat—because of jungle fever?

HAROLD
I could eat a raw baby crocodile.

[*Turning to* LOOSELEAF *crassly*]

The way to get your wife back is in bed. Do such a job on her that she'll be lucky if she can crawl around on all fours.

[*To* PENELOPE]

We're starving. Do you mind?

[PENELOPE *exits dumbly, detesting the word "scrog," which she has never heard before*]

She had two lovers, by the way.

[LOOSELEAF *starts to laugh again, stops the laugh as* HAROLD *glowers*]

LOOSELEAF
Excuse me.

HAROLD
One of them is the doctor, whose weapons are compassion, unselfishness, peacefulness—maudlin concern.

LOOSELEAF
Huh.

HAROLD
He and his love are like a retiarius. Do you know what a retiarius is?

LOOSELEAF
He's a kind of gladiator who fights with a knife and a net and doesn't wear anything but a jockstrap.

HAROLD

[*Amazed*]

How do you know that?

LOOSELEAF
You told me.

HAROLD
When?

LOOSELEAF
When we were up in the tree so long—with the bats.

HAROLD
Oh. I'd forgotten.

LOOSELEAF
Fourteen times you told me. I counted.

HAROLD
Really?

LOOSELEAF
You'd get this funny look in your eyes, and I'd say to myself, "Oh, Jesus—he's going to tell me what a retiarius is again."

HAROLD

[*Acknowledging a flaw in a manly way*]

Sorry.

[PENELOPE *enters, is about to speak.* HAROLD *stops her with a raised finger*]

Let me guess—breakfast is served?

PENELOPE
No.

HAROLD
What then?

PENELOPE
I do not wish to be *scrogged*—ever. I never heard that word, but when I heard it, I knew it was one thing I never wanted to have happen to me.

HAROLD
That's what you're *supposed* to say.

PENELOPE
This is not a coy deception. I do not want to be scrogged. I want love. I want tenderness.

HAROLD
You don't *know* you want. That's the way God *built* you!

PENELOPE
I will not be scrogged. I remember one time I saw you wrench a hook from the throat of a fish with a pair of pliers, and you promised me that the fish couldn't feel.

HAROLD
It couldn't!

PENELOPE
I'd like to have the expert opinion of the fish—along with yours.

HAROLD

[*Shaking his head*]

Fish can't feel.

PENELOPE
Well, *I* can. Some injuries, spiritual or physical, can
be excruciating to me. I'm not a silly carhop any more.

[*An unexpected, minor insight*]

Maybe you're right about fish. When I was a carhop, I
didn't feel much more than a fish would. But I've been
sensitized. I have ideas now—and solid information. I
know a lot more now—and a lot of it has to do with
you.

HAROLD

[*Sensing danger*]

Such as? . . .

PENELOPE
The whole concept of heroism—and its sexual roots.

HAROLD
Tell me about its sexual roots.

PENELOPE
It's complicated and I don't want to go into it now,
because it's bound to sound insulting—even though
nobody means for anybody to be insulted. It's just the
truth.

HAROLD
I like the truth. I wouldn't be alive today if I weren't
one of the biggest fans truth ever had.

PENELOPE
Well—part of it is that heroes basically hate home and
never stay there very long, and make awful messes
while they're there.

HAROLD
Go on.

PENELOPE

[*Blurting*]

And they have very mixed feelings about women. They
hate them in a way. One reason they like war so much
is that they can capture enemy women and not have to
make love to them slowly and gently. They can *scrog*
them, as you say—

[*Pause*]

for revenge.

HAROLD
You learned this in some college course?

PENELOPE
I learned a lot of things in college. Actually—it was
Norbert who told me that.

HAROLD

[*Darkly*]

The doctor.

PENELOPE
Yes.

HAROLD
And what is his most cherished possession?

PENELOPE

[*Not sensing the drift of the conversation*]

His most cherished possession? His violin, I guess.

HAROLD
And he keeps it in his apartment?

PENELOPE

[*Still at sea*]

Yes.

HAROLD
And no one's there now?

PENELOPE
I don't think so.

HAROLD
That's too bad. I would rather have him at home—to *see* what I'm going to do.

PENELOPE

[*Suddenly catching on, sick with fear*]

What are you going to do?

HAROLD
He did his best to destroy my most precious possession, which is the high opinion women have of me. I'm now going to even that score. I'm going to break in his door and I'm going to smash his violin.

PENELOPE
No you're not!

HAROLD
Why not?

PENELOPE
Because if you do—I'll *leave* you.

HAROLD

[*Promptly and emotionlessly*]

Goodbye.

[*Blackout*]

SCENE TWO

SPOTLIGHT comes up on VON
KONIGSWALD and WANDA JUNE,
dressed as before. They have become
close friends.

WANDA JUNE
We have this new club up here in Heaven.

VON KONIGSWALD
Yes, we do.

WANDA JUNE
We only have two members so far, but it's growing all the
time.

VON KONIGSWALD
We have enough for a shuffleboard team. In Heaven,
shuffleboard is everything. Hitler plays shuffleboard.

WANDA JUNE
Albert Einstein plays shuffleboard.

VON KONIGSWALD
Mozart plays shuffleboard.

WANDA JUNE
Lewis Carroll, who wrote *Alice in Wonderland,* plays
shuffleboard.

VON KONIGSWALD
Jack the Ripper plays shuffleboard.

WANDA JUNE
Walt Disney, who gave us *Snow White and the Seven
Dwarfs,* plays shuffleboard. Jesus Christ plays shuffleboard.

VON. KONIGSWALD
It was almost worth the trip—to find out that Jesus Christ
in Heaven was just another guy, playing shuffleboard. I
like his sense of humor, though—you know? He's got
a blue-and-gold warm-up jacket he wears. You know
what it says on the back? "Pontius Pilate Athletic Club."
Most people don't get it. Most people think there really
is a Pontius Pilate Athletic Club.

WANDA JUNE
We're going to have jackets, aren't we?

VON KONIGSWALD
You bet! "The Harold Ryan Fan Club." Pink, eh? With
a yellow streak up the back.

[BOTH *laugh*]

We got very good tailor shops up here. They'll make
you any kind of uniform, any kind of sweatsuit you
want. Judas Iscariot—he's got this black jacket with a
skull and crossbones over the heart. He walks around

all hunched over, and he never looks anybody in the eye, and written on the back of his jacket are the words, "Go take a flying—

[WANDA JUNE *punches him in the ribs*]

leap at the moon."

[MILDRED, HAROLD'*s third wife, enters. She is voluptuous, blowzy, tough—about forty-five. She has trouble with alcohol.* VON KONIGSWALD *is expecting her*]

Aha! Hello! You're Mildred, right?

MILDRED
I heard you were looking for me.

VON KONIGSWALD
You were Harold Ryan's third wife. Right?

MILDRED
Yes.

VON KONIGSWALD
You want to join the Harold Ryan Fan Club? Wear a pink jacket with a yellow streak up the back?

MILDRED
Do I have to? Who's the little girl?

WANDA JUNE
Mr. Ryan just borrowed my birthday cake. I don't really know him.

MILDRED
Thought you were another wife, maybe.

WANDA JUNE
I'm only *ten* years old.

MILDRED
That's what he wanted—a ten-year-old wife. He'd come home from a war or a safari, and he'd wind up talking to the little kids.

WANDA JUNE
Won't you *please* join our club? Please?

MILDRED
Honey—Alcoholics Anonymous takes all the time I've got—and Harold Ryan is an individual I would rather forget. He drove me to drink. He drove his first two wives to drink.

VON KONIGSWALD
Because he was cruel?

MILDRED

[*Covering* WANDA JUNE's *little ears*]

Premature ejaculation.

VON KONIGSWALD
Ach soooooooooooo.

MILDRED
No grown woman is a fan of premature ejaculation.
Harold would come home trumpeting and roaring. He
would kick the furniture with his boots, spit into corners
and the fireplace. He would make me presents of stuffed
fish and helmets with holes in them. He would tell me
that he had now earned the reward that only a woman
could give him, and he'd tear off my clothes. He would
carry me into the bedroom, telling me to scream and
kick my feet. That was very important to him. I did it.
I tried to be a good wife. He told me to imagine a herd
of stampeding water buffalo. I couldn't do that, but I
pretended I did. It was all over—ten seconds after he'd
said the word "buffalo." Then he'd zip up his pants, and
go outside, and tell true war stories to the little kids.
Any little kids.

VON KONIGSWALD
That is sad.

MILDRED

  [*Blankly*]

Is it?

  [*Pause*]

I have this theory about why men kill each other and
break things.

VON KONIGSWALD
Ja?

MILDRED
Never mind. It's a dumb theory. I was going to say it
was all sexual . . . but everything is sexual . . . but
alcohol.

[*Making peace sign*]

Peace.

VON KONIGSWALD & WANDA JUNE

[*Making peace signs*]

Peace.

[*Blackout*]

SCENE THREE

SILENCE. Darkness.

WOODY WOODPECKER VOICE
Ha ha ha *ha* ha!

[*Pistol shot*]

You got me, pal.

[*Silence. A baby cries. Silence. The lights come up*]

LOOSELEAF
Go to the *funeral?*

HAROLD
Of course! Not only go to it but go to it in full uniform!
Rent a uniform!

LOOSELEAF
That's against the law, isn't it? I can't wear a uniform
anymore.

HAROLD
Wear your uniform and every decoration, and let them
despise you, if they dare.

LOOSELEAF
Alice would be absolutely tear-ass.

HAROLD
When I was a naive young recruit in Spain, I used to
wonder why soldiers bayoneted oil paintings, shot the
noses off of statues and defecated into grand pianos. I
now understand: It was to teach civilians the deepest sort
of respect for men in uniform—uncontrollable fear.

[*He raises his glass*]

To our women.

LOOSELEAF
I didn't know we had any women left.

HAROLD
The world is teeming with women—ours to enjoy.

LOOSELEAF
Every time I start thinking like that I get the clap.

[*Lion doorbell roars*]

HAROLD

[*Going to the door*]

This could be my next wife.

[*He admits* HERB SHUTTLE, *who carries a bouquet of
roses*]

SHUTTLE

[*Puzzled by* HAROLD]

Hello.

HAROLD
How are you, honeybunch?

SHUTTLE
Is Penelope in?

HAROLD
The posies are for *her?*

SHUTTLE
I wanted to apologize.

HAROLD
You've come to the right man.

SHUTTLE
I forgot my vacuum cleaner.

HAROLD
I forget mine for years on end.

SHUTTLE

[*Suddenly realizing who* HAROLD *is*]

Oh my God—

[*Pause.* SHUTTLE *points*]

And *you* are Looseleaf Harper.

LOOSELEAF
Hi.

[SHUTTLE *faints*]

HAROLD

[*Crowing*]

It's what I've dreamed of all my life, Looseleaf! To have a grown man realize who I was—and *faint!*

[*To audience*]

End of Act Two.

[*Blackout*]

ACT THREE

MILDRED enters drunkenly up aisle, sits
precariously on apron of stage and
speaks to audience.

MILDRED
Two days later. The afternoon of the day of Looseleaf
Harper's mother-in-law's funeral. You got it? Two days
later.

[*Pause*]

You know what happened in *Heaven* today? There was
a tornado. I'm not kidding you—there was a Goddamn
tornado. Tore up fifty-six houses, a dance pavilion and
a Ferris wheel. Drove a shuffleboard stick clear through
a telephone pole. Nobody got killed. Nobody ever gets
killed. They just bounce around a lot. Then they get
up—and start playing shuffleboard again.

[*Pause*]

I never saw a tornado when I was alive, and I grew up
in Oklahoma. There's this big, black, funnel-shaped
cloud. Sounds like a railroad train without the whistle. I

had to come to Heaven to see a thing like that. A lot of
people got photographs.

[*Pause*]

After the tornado was over, a man had some film left and
he wanted to take pictures of me—to use up the *roll*. I
don't like people who go around taking pictures of
everything. Nothing's real to some people unless they've
got photographs.

[*Pause*]

Two days later—right?

[*She exits clumsily, the way she came. Silence. Lights
come up on the living room, which has become a pigpen.*
LOOSELEAF, HAROLD, SHUTTLE *and* PAUL *sit around
a dinner of nearly raw beefsteak set on the coffee table.*
LOOSELEAF *wears an ill-fitting uniform, which he has
rented*]

LOOSELEAF
I told you the uniform wouldn't help.

HAROLD
It helped more than you know. Down deep, people were
deeply affected.

LOOSELEAF
You keep on saying "deep" and "deeply." I wish
something good would happen on the surface sometime.

SHUTTLE
I can't get over how you guys are my friends. Harold
Ryan and Looseleaf Harper are my friends.

HAROLD
Our pleasure.

SHUTTLE
Eight years you guys were together—through thick and
thin.

HAROLD
For seven and a half of those years we were heavily
drugged—or we would have been home long before now,
believe me. We were saved from starvation by the
Lupi-Loopo Indians, who fed us a strange blue soup.

SHUTTLE
Blue soup.

HAROLD
It sapped our will—made us peaceful and unenterprising.
It was a form of chemical castration. We became two
more sleepy Indians.

LOOSELEAF

[*To* PAUL]

So, kid—how they hanging? Or don't you *say* that to a
little kid?

HAROLD
He's a *man*.

    [*To* PAUL]

Tell him you're a *man*.

PAUL
I'm a man.

HAROLD
We've got to do something to make this boy's voice change. I wonder if we couldn't get bull balls somewhere, and fry 'em up.

    [*To* PAUL]

Still miss your mother?

PAUL

[*Weakly*]

No.

HAROLD
You're free to go to her, if you want. If you'd rather
be a woman and run with the women, just say the
word.

SHUTTLE
Are we really going to find out where the elephants go to
die?

HAROLD
I'd rather go to Viet Nam.

SHUTTLE
Would somebody please pass me the catsup?

HAROLD
What you say is, "Pass the fucking catsup."

SHUTTLE
Pass the fucking catsup.

[LOOSELEAF *gives it to him.* SHUTTLE *dumps catsup on
his steak*]

I keep thinking about Africa—and the elephants.

LOOSELEAF
I don't think I'll go.

HAROLD
Of course you'll go! You're going to fly the helicopter.

LOOSELEAF
I dunno.

HAROLD
You're so *low!* Look at that beautiful red meat. You haven't touched it.

LOOSELEAF
Sorry. At least you've got a place to come back to. I don't have a place to come *back* to anymore.

HAROLD
All the more reason to go to Africa.

LOOSELEAF
I dunno. You know.

   [*Pause*]

I used to really love that Alice. Do you know that?

HAROLD
You know her for what she is now—garbage.

LOOSELEAF
I dunno.

HAROLD
She was always a rotten wife! She was against everything
manly you ever wanted to do.

[*To* SHUTTLE]

He was the most daring test pilot in the country at one
time, and his wife made him quit. She made him become
a life insurance salesman instead.

SHUTTLE
I'd think any woman worth her salt would be proud to
be married to a test pilot. I know I would.

LOOSELEAF
She *tried* to like it. She was a very nervous woman.

SHUTTLE
I could tell that at the funeral.

[*To* PAUL]

Would you please pass the fucking catsup again? Was it
dangerous testing planes?

LOOSELEAF
I dunno. Who knows? You know—you're up there, and
you're in some plane nobody ever flew before. You put
her into a dive, and everything starts screaming and
shaking, and maybe some pipe breaks and squirts oil or
gasoline or hydraulic fluid in your face. You wonder how
the hell you ever got in such a mess, and then you pull
back on the controls, and you black out for a couple of

seconds. When you come to, everything's usually fairly
okay—except maybe you threw up all over yourself. It's
just another job, but you try and tell Alice that.

HAROLD
Insurance!

SHUTTLE
You actually *sold* insurance?

LOOSELEAF
I tried.

[*Indicating* HAROLD]

I sold *him* some. That was the only insurance I ever sold.

[*Hyena doorbell laughs*]

SHUTTLE
What an awful sound!

HAROLD
Get used to it.

[*To* PAUL]

Back door, Paul.

[PAUL *exits to the kitchen. To* SHUTTLE]

It's possible, of course, that you'll *die* in Africa.

SHUTTLE
I've considered that.

HAROLD
Selling vacuum cleaners isn't the best preparation you could have.

SHUTTLE
I just want one true adventure before I die.

HAROLD
That can be arranged.

> [PAUL *appears at the mouth of the doorway. He has something amazing to announce*]

PAUL
Dad?

HAROLD
Who was it?

PAUL
It's Mom.

> [*He steps aside.* PENELOPE *appears.* HAROLD *and* SHUTTLE *stand,* HAROLD *angrily*]

LOOSELEAF

> [*Openly, cheerfully*]

Hi, Penelope.

HAROLD

[*To* LOOSELEAF]

Shut up, you ninny!

[*To* PENELOPE]

You were never to come here again—for any reason whatsoever!

PENELOPE
I came for my clothes.

HAROLD
Sneaking in the back door.

PENELOPE
I rang. It seemed like the proper door for a servile, worthless organism to use.

HAROLD
Your clothes are at the city dump by now. Perhaps you can get a map from the Department of Sanitation.

PENELOPE
I came for Paul as well.

HAROLD
If he wants to go.

PENELOPE
You took him to the funeral, I hear.

HAROLD
He'd never seen a corpse. He's seen a dozen now.

PENELOPE
A *dozen?*

HAROLD
It's a big and busy funeral home.

PENELOPE

[*To* PAUL]

Did you like it, dear?

HAROLD
It isn't a matter of *liking*. It's a matter of getting *used* to death—as a perfectly natural thing. Would you mind leaving? No woman ever walks out on Harold Ryan, and then comes back—for anything.

PENELOPE
Unless she has nerve.

HAROLD
More nerve than the doctor, I must admit. He hasn't been home for two days. Has he suddenly lost interest in sleep and color television—and the violin?

PENELOPE
He knows you shattered his violin.

HAROLD
I'm dying to hear of his reaction. The thrill of smashing something isn't in the smashing, but in the owner's reactions.

PENELOPE
He cried.

HAROLD
About a broomstick and a cigar box—and the attenuated intestines of an alley cat.

PENELOPE
Two hundred years old.

HAROLD
He feels awful *loss*—which was precisely my intention.

PENELOPE

[*Moving toward the violin, and, incidentally, placing herself much closer to* SHUTTLE]

He had hoped that someone would be playing it still—two hundred years from now.

HAROLD

[*Echoing, expressing the futility of such long-term expectations*]

Hope.

[*He spots the vacuum cleaner, probes it with his toe, asks* SHUTTLE *with seriousness*]

Do you hope with all your heart that someone will be using this vacuum cleaner two hundred years from now?

[SHUTTLE *starts to answer, but stops, supposing that he is being made sport of*]

Fifty years?

SHUTTLE
You're making a joke.

HAROLD

[*Not joking*]

I'm interested in long-term expectations.

SHUTTLE

[*Flatly, protecting his dignity*]

It's engineered to last about fifteen years.

HAROLD

[*Downstage center, addressing the civilized world*]

Things. Oh—you silly people and your things. Things, things, things.

PENELOPE

[*To* SHUTTLE, *as* HAROLD *reflects majestically on the emptiness of materialism*]

You and Harold are *friends?*

SHUTTLE

[*Revealing how mixed and worried his feelings are*]

He's the most wonderful guy I ever met, Penelope. He's the most complicated guy I ever met. I can't believe it, but he's going to take me to Africa with him.

HAROLD
Things.

PENELOPE
You feel I've done a dreadful thing—leaving him?

SHUTTLE

[*Almost hypnotized*]

If *I* were married to him, *I* sure wouldn't walk out.

HAROLD

[*Directly to the audience*]

Never mind the condition of your body and your spirit! Look after your things, your things!

PENELOPE

[*To* LOOSELEAF]

And you, Colonel? Let me guess: You don't know.

LOOSELEAF
I dunno.

HAROLD

[*To the audience*]

Go live in a safe-deposit box—with your things.

LOOSELEAF
Jesus—I wouldn't want to be married to *him*. You *know?*

HAROLD
What's this?

LOOSELEAF
I wouldn't want to be married to *me*. We're too crazy.
You know?

HAROLD
In what way, pray tell?

LOOSELEAF
I didn't like that violin thing. That was sad.

HAROLD
Tit for tat—as simple as that.

LOOSELEAF
You never *played* a violin.

HAROLD
You *did?*

LOOSELEAF
Yeah. I practically forgot. But after you busted that thing,
I got to thinking, "Jesus—maybe I'll start the violin
again." That was a mean, childish thing—busting that
violin. That didn't just belong to Woodly. That belonged
to *everybody*. Maybe he would have sold it to me, and
I could have some fun. Then I could sell it to somebody
else, and he could have some fun. After you busted the
violin, boy, and Penelope walked out, I thought to
myself, "Jesus—who could blame her?"

HAROLD
Maybe it's time *you* got out.

LOOSELEAF
Me?

HAROLD
You.

LOOSELEAF
Okay.

[*Pause*]

Okay.

HAROLD
You're an imbecile.

LOOSELEAF
I know you think that.

HAROLD
Everybody thinks that.

LOOSELEAF
Anybody who'd drop an atom bomb on a city has to be pretty dumb.

HAROLD
The one direct, decisive, intelligent act of your life!

LOOSELEAF

[*Shaking his head*]

I don't think so.

[*Pause*]

It *could* have been.

HAROLD
If what?

LOOSELEAF
If I *hadn't* done it. If I'd said to myself, "Screw it. I'm going to let all those people down there live."

HAROLD
They were enemies. We were at war.

LOOSELEAF
Yeah, Jesus—but wars would be a lot better, I think, if guys would say to themselves sometimes, "Jesus—I'm not going to do that to the enemy. That's *too* much." You could have been the manufacturer of that violin there, even though you don't know how to make a violin, just by not busting it up. I could have been the father of all those people in Nagasaki, and the mother, too, just by not dropping the bomb.

   [*Pause*]

I sent 'em to Heaven instead—and I don't think there *is* one.

HAROLD
Goodbye, Looseleaf.

   [LOOSELEAF *walks around and gathers his things*]

LOOSELEAF
So long, you guys.

PENELOPE
What will you do, Colonel?

LOOSELEAF
I dunno. Marry the first whore who's nice to me, I guess. Get a job in a motorcycle shop. So long, you guys.

[PENELOPE *kisses* LOOSELEAF. *Everybody but* HAROLD *acknowledges his departure in some way.* HAROLD *turns his back.* LOOSELEAF *exits, closes door. Silence*]

SHUTTLE
Who's going to fly our helicopter now?

HAROLD

[*Blackly, tautly*]

What?

SHUTTLE
We got to get another pilot.

HAROLD
For what?

SHUTTLE
For *Africa.*

HAROLD
Do you really think that Harold Ryan would go to Africa with a vacuum cleaner salesman?

SHUTTLE
You *invited* me.

HAROLD
To make an ass of yourself.

SHUTTLE
What went wrong?

HAROLD
We're ahead of schedule, that's all. You're finding out
here what you would have found out in Africa—that you
are a rabbit, born to be eaten alive.

SHUTTLE
Gee whiz—

HAROLD
It would have been fun to see you drop your rifle and run
the first time an elephant charged us.

SHUTTLE
I wouldn't drop my gun.

HAROLD
You're hollow, like a woman.

SHUTTLE
I'm smarter than Looseleaf.

HAROLD
He can shoot! He can hold his ground! He can attack!
You're in your proper profession right now—sucking
up dirt for frumpish housewives, closet drunkards every
one.

SHUTTLE

   [*Close to tears*]

How do you *know* how I'd act in Africa?

HAROLD
Look how you're acting now! This is a moment of truth, and you're almost crying. Slug me!

SHUTTLE
You're my buddy.

HAROLD
Out! Out!

SHUTTLE
No matter what you say to me, I still think you're the greatest guy I ever knew.

HAROLD
Out!

SHUTTLE
You—you aren't going to have any *friends* left, if you don't watch out.

HAROLD
Thank God!

[*He propels* SHUTTLE *out the door and slams it. He faces* PENELOPE *and* PAUL, *speaks with malicious calm*]

Well—what have we here? A family.

PENELOPE
Almost a Christmas scene.

HAROLD
Goodbye, goodbye, goodbye.

PENELOPE
Just one favor.

HAROLD
Money? There's plenty of that. Mildred got the brewery.
You'll probably get the baseball team.

PENELOPE
I want you to tell me that you loved me once.

> [HAROLD *is about to dismiss this request majestically,*
> *but* PENELOPE *cuts him off with a sharp, dangerous*
> *warning*]

I *mean* it! I must have that, and so must Paul. Tell him
that he was conceived in love, even though you hate me
now. Tell both of us that somewhere in our lives was
love.

> [HAROLD *experiments inwardly with responses of*
> *various kinds, obviously saying them to himself,*
> *directing himself with his hands. Nothing quite*
> *satisfies him*]

HAROLD
Testimonials of that sort are—are beyond my range. I
don't do them well.

> [*Sincerely, not liking to fail in any area*]

That's a failing, I know.

PENELOPE

[*Accepting this ruefully*]

I see.

PAUL
I don't care. I don't care if there was love or not.
That's all right. I'm going to go to my room and close
the door. I don't want to *hear* any more.

[PAUL *exits wretchedly to his room*]

HAROLD
See how you've upset him. He was so merry and hale
before you came home.

PENELOPE
How unhappy he's going to be—alone in his room.

HAROLD
He'll play with his rifle, I expect. That will cheer him
up.

PENELOPE
Rifle?

HAROLD
I bought him a twenty-two yesterday—on the way home
from Hamburger Heaven. And where is the good doctor?
Have you two feathered a love nest somewhere?

PENELOPE
He's in East St. Louis with his mother—visiting an aunt.

HAROLD
Last I heard, his mother was going alone.

PENELOPE
He's *afraid* of you, Harold. He knew you'd want to fight him. He doesn't know anything about fighting. He *hates* pain.

HAROLD
And you, a supposedly healthy woman, do not detest him for his cowardice?

PENELOPE
It seems highly intelligent to me.

HAROLD
What kind of a country has this become? The men wear beads and refuse to fight—and the women *adore* them. America's days of greatness are over. It has drunk the blue soup.

PENELOPE
Blue soup?

HAROLD
An Indian narcotic we were forced to drink. It put us in a haze—a honey-colored haze which was lavender around the edge. We laughed, we sang, we snoozed. When a bird called, we answered back. Every living thing was our brother or our sister, we thought. Looseleaf stepped on

a cockroach six inches long, and we cried. We had a
funeral that went on for five days—for the *cockroach!*
I sang "Oh Promise Me." Can you imagine? Where the
hell did I ever learn the words to "Oh Promise Me"?
Looseleaf delivered a lecture on maintenance procedures
for the hydraulic system of a B-36. All the time we were
drinking more blue soup, more blue soup! Never stopped
drinking blue soup. Blue soup all the time. We'd go out
after food in that honey-colored haze, and everything
that was edible had a penumbra of lavender.

PENELOPE
Sounds quite beautiful.

HAROLD

   [*Angered*]

Beautiful, you say? It wasn't life, it wasn't death—it
wasn't anything!

   [*Anger still mounting*]

Beautiful? Seven years gone—

   [*Snapping his fingers*]

like that, like *that!* Seven years of silliness and random
dreams! Seven years of nothingness, when there could
have been so *much!*

PENELOPE
Like what?

HAROLD

[*Becoming dangerously physical, seizing a battle-ax*]

Action! Interaction! Give and take! Challenge and response!

[*He splits a coffee table with the ax*]

PAUL

[*Rushing in with his .22 rifle at a high port arms*]

Mom?

HAROLD
What's this?

[PAUL *wilts instantly, attempts to make his rifle inconspicuous, harmless, meaningless*]

What's this?

PAUL
Nothing.

HAROLD
That's a *rifle* you have?

PAUL
No.

HAROLD
Of course it is. Is it loaded?

PAUL
No.

HAROLD
Open the bolt!

[PAUL *obeys. A cartridge pops out*]

That's a cartridge, if I'm not mistaken. Gunpowder, bullet, cartridge case, and fulminate of mercury percussion cap—all set to go.

PAUL
I was cleaning it.

HAROLD
Pick up that cartridge and slip it back into the chamber— where it belongs.

PAUL
Gee whiz, Dad—

HAROLD
Welcome to manhood, you little sparrowfart! Load that gun!

PAUL

[*Bleatingly*]

Dad—

HAROLD
Too late! It's man to man now. Protecting your mother
from me, are you? Protect her!

PENELOPE
He's a child!

HAROLD
With an iron penis three feet long. Load it, boy.

PENELOPE
You're begging him to *kill* you?

HAROLD
If he thinks he's man enough.

PENELOPE

[*Amazed by sudden insight*]

That's really what you want. You become furious when
people won't make you dead.

HAROLD
I'm teaching my son to be a man.

PENELOPE
So he can kill you. You hate your own life that much. You
beg for a hero to kill you.

HAROLD
I plan to live one hundred years!

PENELOPE
No you don't.

HAROLD
If that's the case—what's to prevent my killing myself?

PENELOPE
Honor, I suppose.

HAROLD
What a handsome word.

PENELOPE

[*Wonderingly*]

But it's all balled up in your head with death. The highest
honor is death. When you talk of these animals, one
by one, you don't just talk of killing them. You *honored*
them with death. Harold—it is not honor to be killed.

HAROLD
If you've lived a good life, fought well—

PENELOPE
It's still just death, the absence of life—no honor at all.
It's worse than the blue soup by far—that nothingness.
To you, though, it's the honor that crowns them all.

HAROLD
May I continue with the rearing of my son?

   [*To* PAUL]

Load that gun!

   [PAUL *shakes his head*]

Load it!

   [PAUL *refuses*]

Then *speak,* by God! Can you fight with words?

PAUL
I don't want to fight you.

HAROLD
Get mad! Tell me you don't like the way I treat your
mother! Tell me you wish I'd never come home!

PAUL

   [*Weakly*]

It's your house, Dad.

HAROLD

   [*Throwing up his hands*]

Everybody simply *evaporates!*

[*Including the audience, inviting it to share his indignation*]

There are great issues to be fought out here—or to be argued, at least. The enemy, the champion of all who oppose me, is in East St. Louis with his mother and his aunt! I have so far done battle with a woman and a child and a violin.

PENELOPE
The old heroes are going to have to get used to this, Harold—the new heroes who refuse to fight. They're trying to save the planet. There's no time for battle, no point to battle anymore.

HAROLD
I feel mocked, insulted, with no sort of satisfaction in prospect. We don't have to fight with steel. I can fight with words. I'm not an inarticulate ape, you know, who grabs a rock for want of a vocabulary. Call him up in East St. Louis, Penelope. Tell him to come here.

PENELOPE
No.

HAROLD

[*Emptily, turning away*]

No.

[*Pause. He contemplates* PAUL]

And my son, the only son of Harold Ryan—he's going to grow up to be a vanisher, too?

PENELOPE
I don't know. I hope he never hunts. I hope he never kills another human being.

HAROLD

[*To* PAUL, *quietly*]

You hope this, too?

PAUL
I don't know what I hope. But I don't think you care what I hope, anyway. You don't know me.

[*Indicating* PENELOPE]

You don't know her, either. I don't think you know anybody. You talk to everybody just the same.

HAROLD
I'm talking to you *gently* now.

PAUL
Yeah. But it's going to get loud again.

PENELOPE
He's right, Harold. To you, we're simply pieces in a game —this one labeled "woman," that one labeled "son." There is no piece labeled "enemy" and you are confused.

[*Lion doorbell rings.* PAUL *goes to answer it*]

HAROLD
There won't be anybody out there. That's the new style: nobody anywhere.

[PAUL, *aghast, admits* NORBERT WOODLY. WOODLY *is high as a kite on his own adrenalin*]

PENELOPE

[*Aghast, chokingly*]

Get out of here.

WOODLY
It's really that bad?

[*He comes farther into the room, bravely*]

PENELOPE
You fool, you fool.

WOODLY
Oh—look at the poor, crucified violin, would you?

HAROLD
It died for your sins.

WOODLY
This little corpse is intended as a lesson?

HAROLD
There's a certain amount of information there.

WOODLY
Lest we forget how cruel you are.

PENELOPE

[*Moving to the telephone*]

I'm going to call the police.

HAROLD

[*Frighteningly*]

Don't!

WOODLY
I agree.

[*Closes door.* PENELOPE *backs away from the phone, drifts toward* PAUL, *who still holds his rifle*]

HAROLD
This is man to man.

WOODLY
It's healer to killer. Is that the same thing?

HAROLD
What brought you back?

WOODLY
The same hairy, humorless old gods who move you from hither to yon. "Honor," if you like.

HAROLD

[*To* PENELOPE]

He's a champion after all.

WOODLY
Of the corpses and cripples you create for our instruction —when all we can learn from them is this: how cruel you are.

PENELOPE
This is suicide.

[*To* PAUL]

Go get the police.

HAROLD
Stop!

[PAUL *stops*]

There's going to be no bloodshed here. I know how he'll fight—the only way he can fight: with words. The truth.

[*To* WOODLY]

Am I correct?

WOODLY
Yes.

HAROLD
I can defeat him with anything from flavored toothpicks to siege howitzers. But he got it into his little head that he could come here and demolish Harold Ryan with words. The *truth!* Correct?

WOODLY
Correct.

HAROLD
What an hallucination!

   [*He laughs*]

Oh, dear, dear, dear, dear. Oh dearie me.

WOODLY
You haven't heard me yet.

HAROLD
You intend to crack my eardrums with your voice? Will I bleed from my every orifice? Who will clean up this awful mess?

WOODLY
We'll find out now, won't we?

PENELOPE
No, we won't. No matter how it begins, it will end in death.

Because it always does. Isn't that always how it ends, Harold—in *death?*

HAROLD
There has to be a threat of some sort, nobility of some sort, glamor of some sort, sport of some sort. These elements are lacking.

WOODLY
You're a filthy, rotten bastard.

HAROLD

[*Pretending to be wounded*]

Oooooo. That hurt.

WOODLY
You're old—so old.

HAROLD
Now who's being cruel?

WOODLY
A living fossil! Like the cockroaches and the horseshoe crabs.

HAROLD
We *do* survive, don't we? You're going to have to apologize, of course, for calling me a bastard. That's a matter of form—not allowing you or anybody to call me a bastard. No rush about that. Just remember to apologize sometime soon.

[PENELOPE *takes the rifle from* PAUL]

WOODLY
You're a son of a bitch.

HAROLD
Yes—well—uh—that's another one of those statements
which more or less automatically requires an apology.
Whenever you feel like it. It's sort of like turning off an
alarm clock that's ringing loudly. Your apology turns
off the alarm.

PENELOPE

[*Leveling the gun*]

I'm turning off the alarm. I'm turning off everything.

HAROLD
Ah! The lady is armed.

PENELOPE
I want you to get out of here, Norbert. Harold—I want
you to sit down in the chair, and not lift a finger until
Norbert is gone.

HAROLD

[*To* WOODLY]

Whoever has the gun, you see, gets to tell everybody else
exactly what to do. It's the American way.

PENELOPE
I *mean* it!

HAROLD
Then you'd better fix your bayonet, because there aren't
any bullets in the gun.

PENELOPE

[*To* PAUL]

Where's the bullet?

[PAUL *makes no move to help*]

HAROLD
Help your mother find the bullet.

PENELOPE

[*To* PAUL, *pointing to the floor*]

There it is. Give it to me.

[PAUL *obeys*]

How do I load?

HAROLD

[*To* PAUL]

Load it for her.

[PAUL *shakily obeys*]

Cock it, too.

[PAUL *obeys*]

Give it to her.

[PAUL *obeys*]

PENELOPE
All right! Am I exceedingly dangerous now?

HAROLD
The National Safety Council would be appalled.

PENELOPE
Then listen to me.

[*Angrily*]

You're both disgusting—with your pride, your pride.

[*To* WOODLY]

I hate you for coming here—like a federal marshal in a western film. I loved you when you stayed away. But here you are now—high noon in the Superbowl! You fool, you fool.

WOODLY
Everything's going to be beautiful.

PENELOPE
You fake! You're no better than the dumbest general in the Pentagon.

[*Pause*]

You're not going to beat Harold. You're not going to beat anybody. You're not going to stay here, either—yammering and taunting until you're most gloriously killed. Go home!

HAROLD
She's right, Norbert—go home.

WOODLY
I haven't said all I have to say.

PENELOPE
Out!

WOODLY
I haven't told you, Harold, how comical I think you are.

HAROLD

[*Hit squarely, absolutely unable to forgive*]

Comical?

PENELOPE

[*To* HAROLD]

Sit down or I'll shoot!

[HAROLD *goes over to her, easily takes the gun away*]

HAROLD
Give me that Goddamn thing! Now get out of here,
or I might kill *you*. Who knows?

PENELOPE

[*Terrified*]

You've killed *women*?

HAROLD
Seventeen of them—eleven by accident. March! Move!

[*To* PAUL]

You, too!

[PENELOPE *and* PAUL *move toward the front door*]

PENELOPE
Norbert—you come, too.

[*To* HAROLD]

Let him go, Harold. Let him go.

HAROLD
Of course he can go—if he'll just go down on his hands

and knees for a moment—and promise me that he does
not find me comical in the least degree.

PENELOPE
Do it, Norbert.

WOODLY
Hands and knees, you say?

HAROLD
And terror, if you don't mind.

PENELOPE
Do it!

WOODLY

[*To* PENELOPE, *simply, decisively, unafraid*]

Goodbye.

HAROLD

[*Before she can protest any more*]

Goodbye! Goodbye!

[*He bellies and bullies* PENELOPE *and* PAUL *out the front door*]

Get the police! No time to lose!

[*He slams the door, turns to* WOODLY]

You're in one hell of a jam. You realize that?

WOODLY
I'm high as a kite.

HAROLD
Glands. You're supposed to be happy when you die. Call me comical again.

WOODLY
You're a clown. You're a clown who *kills*—but you're a clown.

HAROLD
I love you! Have a cigar!

WOODLY

[*Ignoring the cigar*]

Evolution has made you a clown—with a cigar. Simple butchers like you are obsolete!

HAROLD
I'm to be left behind—in primordial ooze?

WOODLY
If you're at home in the ooze, and nowhere else.

HAROLD
This is going to become very physical. Are you prepared for that?

WOODLY
You're not such a creature of the ooze that you'd hurt an unarmed man.

HAROLD
I'm an *honorable* clown?

WOODLY
King Arthur.

HAROLD
You hope.

WOODLY
In any event, I will not beg for mercy.

HAROLD
No quarter asked

   [*Taking a sword*]

No quarter given.

WOODLY
Don't you laugh even *inwardly* at the heroic balderdash you spew?

HAROLD

   [*Offering sword*]

Cut me open. Find out.

WOODLY
I've struck my blow.

HAROLD
With spittle?

WOODLY
I've poisoned you.

HAROLD

[*Pointing at* WOODLY *in horror*]

Lucretia Borgia?

[*Looking around frantically*]

Something I drank or touched?

[*Understanding*]

You refused a cigar. That's it! Potassium cyanide in the humidor! Treacherous lover of peace!

WOODLY
I put a poisoned thought in your head. Even now that poison is seeping into every lobe of your mind. It's saying, "Obsolete, obsolete, obsolete," and, "Clown, clown, clown."

HAROLD
Poison.

WOODLY
You have a very good mind, or I wouldn't have come back.
That mind is now asking itself, cleverly and fairly, "Is
Harold Ryan really a clown?" And the answer is, "Yes."

HAROLD

[*Touching his forehead experimentally*]

I—I really must congratulate you. Something *is* happening
in there.

WOODLY
You can never take yourself seriously again! Look at all
the creatures you've protected us from! Did you shoot
them on the elevator, as they were on their way up here
to eat us alive?

HAROLD

[*Blankly, as though in a dream*]

No.

WOODLY
The magic root you gave me—I had it analyzed. It was
discovered by a Harvard botanist in 1893! He explored
your famous jungle for five years, armed with nothing but
kindness, a talent for languages, and a pocketknife.

HAROLD

[*Blankly*]

I see.

WOODLY
You aren't going to hurt me. You aren't going to hurt anybody any more. Any violent gesture will seem ridiculous —to *yourself!*

HAROLD

[*Quietly*]

Don Quixote.

WOODLY
My violin is avenged!

HAROLD
Something seems to have happened to my self-respect.

WOODLY
And the hell with it. It was so tragically irrelevant, so preposterously misinformed.

HAROLD
The new hero is you.

WOODLY
I hate crowds, and I have no charisma—

HAROLD
You're too modest.

WOODLY
But the new hero will be a man of science and of peace—
like me. He'll disarm you, of course. No more guns, no
more guns.

HAROLD
Was I ever of use?

WOODLY
Never. For when you began to kill for the fun of it, you
became the chief source of agony of mankind.

[HAROLD *picks up the rifle, considers it, offers it to*
WOODLY]

HAROLD
Here. Finish the job.

WOODLY
I'm utterly satisfied.

HAROLD
You're making a mistake. Obsolete old carnivores like me
are most dangerous when wounded. You've wounded
me.

WOODLY
More clowning! Don't you see?

HAROLD
We never quit fighting until we're dead.

WOODLY

You'd be killing a friend. Don't you know how much I
like you?

HAROLD

I'm going to shoot you now.

WOODLY

No!

HAROLD

My self-respect is gone—and my soldier's honor with it.
It is now very easy for me to shoot an unarmed man.

WOODLY

New dignity can be yours—as a *merciful* man. You can
change!

HAROLD

Like the saber-toothed tiger.

WOODLY

[*Sickened*]

Oh God—you're really going to kill me.

HAROLD

It won't hurt as much as the sting of a bumblebee. Heaven
is very much like Paradise, they say. You'll like it there.

WOODLY

Can I beg for mercy—on my knees?

HAROLD
If you want to be found that way.

WOODLY
What is this thing that kills me?

HAROLD
Man, as man was meant to be—a vengeful ape who
murders. He will soon be extinct. It's time, it's time.

WOODLY
Don't shoot.

HAROLD
I've enjoyed being man.

[*He aims the rifle tentatively*]

WOODLY
No.

[*He goes down on his knees*]

No.

HAROLD
Get up.

WOODLY
No.

HAROLD
Have it your way. We'd both be better off dead now.

[HAROLD *begins to squeeze the trigger, falters, lowers the rifle*]

Can't do it.

WOODLY
Thank God.

HAROLD
Crawl home.

[*He turns his back on* WOODLY, *who stands shakily*]

WOODLY
Thank you—for my life.

HAROLD
It's trash now, like mine.

WOODLY
New lives begin!

HAROLD
Somewhere in this city. Not here, not here. Tell Penelope
I loved her—in my clownish way. And Paul. Tell him
to be a healer, by all means.

WOODLY
What are you going to do?

HAROLD
Use the sanitary facilities, if I may.

WOODLY
Leave the rifle here.

HAROLD
I'll put it in Paul's room, where it belongs.

WOODLY
Give me your word of honor that that's all you're going to do.

HAROLD
For what it's worth now, Harold Ryan, the clown, gives his sacred word.

[HAROLD *exits into corridor.* WOODLY *looks after him helplessly, apprehensively. Silence*]

WOODLY
Harold?

[VON KONIGSWALD, MILDRED, *and* WANDA JUNE *enter from the side stealthily.* VON KONIGSWALD *pantomimes that his companions are to be quiet and to listen for something wonderful. All ghosts cup their hands to their ears*]

WOODLY
Harold?

[*There is a shot offstage.* VON KONIGSWALD *is delighted.* MILDRED *is sickened.* WANDA JUNE *is dazed.* WOODLY *collapses in guilt-stricken grief.* HAROLD *enters from the corridor, shaking his head*]

HAROLD
I missed.

[VON KONIGSWALD *expresses disappointment.* MILDRED
covers her face. WANDA JUNE *sucks her thumb*]

The end.

[*Curtain*]

THE EARTH GODS

The Books of

KAHLIL GIBRAN

"His power came from some great reservoir of spiritual life else it could not have been so universal and so potent, but the majesty and beauty of the language with which he clothed it were all his own." — CLAUDE BRAGDON

The Madman · 1918

Twenty Drawings · 1919

The Forerunner · 1920

The Prophet · 1923

Sand and Foam · 1926

Jesus the Son of Man · 1928

The Earth Gods · 1931

The Wanderer · 1932

The Garden of the Prophet · 1933

Prose Poems · 1934

Nymphs of the Valley · 1948

Spirits Rebellious · 1948

A Tear and a Smile · 1950

•ֺ•

Beloved Prophet
The Love Letters of
Kahlil Gibran and Mary Haskell
Edited by Virginia Hilu

This Man from Lebanon—
A Study of Kahlil Gibran
by Barbara Young

PUBLISHED BY ALFRED A. KNOPF

*The twelve illustrations in this volume
are reproduced from original drawings
by the author*

THE EARTH GODS

WHEN the night of the twelfth æon fell,
And silence, the high tide of night, swallowed the
    hills,
The three earth-born gods, the Master Titans of
    life,
Appeared upon the mountains.

Rivers ran about their feet;
The mist floated across their breasts,
And their heads rose in majesty above the world.

Then they spoke, and like distant thunder
Their voices rolled over the plains.

3

FIRST GOD

The wind blows eastward;
I would turn my face to the south,
For the wind crowds my nostrils with the odors of
    dead things.

SECOND GOD

It is the scent of burnt flesh, sweet and bountiful.
I would breathe it.

FIRST GOD

It is the odor of mortality parching upon its own
    faint flame.
Heavily does it hang upon the air,
And like foul breath of the pit
It offends my senses.
I would turn my face to the scentless north.

SECOND GOD

It is the inflamed fragrance of brooding life
4

That I would breathe now and forever.
Gods live upon sacrifice,
Their thirst quenched by blood,
Their hearts appeased with young souls,
Their sinews strengthened by the deathless sighs
Of those who dwell with death;
Their thrones are built upon the ashes of genera-
tions.

FIRST GOD

Weary is my spirit of all there is.
I would not move a hand to create a world
Nor to erase one.

I would not live could I but die,
For the weight of æons is upon me,
And the ceaseless moan of the seas exhausts my
sleep.
Could I but lose the primal aim
And vanish like a wasted sun;
Could I but strip my divinity of its purpose

5

And breathe my immortality into space,
And be no more;
Could I but be consumed and pass from time's mem-
ory
Into the emptiness of nowhere!

THIRD GOD

Listen my brothers, my ancient brothers.
A youth in yonder vale
Is singing his heart to the night.
His lyre is gold and ebony.
His voice is silver and gold.

SECOND GOD

I would not be so vain as to be no more.
I could not but choose the hardest way;
To follow the seasons and support the majesty of
the years;
To sow the seed and to watch it thrust through the
soil;
To call the flower from its hiding place
6

And give it strength to nestle its own life,
And then to pluck it when the storm laughs in the
 forest;
To raise man from secret darkness,
Yet keep his roots clinging to the earth;
To give him thirst for life, and make death his cup-
 bearer;
To endow him with love that waxeth with pain,
And exalts with desire, and increases with longing,
And fadeth away with the first embrace;
To girdle his nights with dreams of higher days,
And infuse his days with visions of blissful nights,
And yet to confine his days and his nights
To their immutable resemblance;
To make his fancy like the eagle of the mountain,
And his thought as the tempests of the seas,
And yet to give him hands slow in decision,
And feet heavy with deliberation;
To give him gladness that he may sing before us,
And sorrow that he may call unto us,
And then to lay him low,

When the earth in her hunger cries for food;
To raise his soul high above the firmament
That he may foretaste our tomorrow,
And to keep his body groveling in the mire
That he may not forget his yesterday.

Thus shall we rule man unto the end of time,
Governing the breath that began with his mother's
      crying,
And ends with the lamentation of his children.

FIRST GOD

My heart thirsts, yet I would not drink the faint
    blood of a feeble race,
For the cup is tainted, and the vintage therein is
    bitter to my mouth.
Like thee I have kneaded the clay and fashioned it
    to breathing forms
That crept out of my dripping fingers unto the
    marshes and the hills.

8

Like thee I have kindled the dark depths of begin-
ning life
And watched it crawl from caves to rocky heights.
Like thee I have summoned spring and laid the
beauty thereof
For a lure that seizes youth and binds it to generate
and multiply.
Like thee I have led man from shrine to shrine,
And turned his mute fear of things unseen
To tremulous faith in us, the unvisited and the un-
known.
Like thee I have ridden the wild tempest over his
head
That he might bow before us,
And shaken the earth beneath him until he cried
unto us;
And like thee, led the savage ocean against his
nested isle,
Till he hath died calling upon us.
All this have I done, and more.
And all that I have done is empty and vain.

9

Vain is the waking and empty is the sleep,
And thrice empty and vain is the dream.

THIRD GOD

Brothers, my august brothers,
Down in the myrtle grove
A girl is dancing to the moon,
A thousand dew-stars are in her hair,
About her feet a thousand wings.

SECOND GOD

We have planted man, our vine, and tilled the soil
In the purple mist of the first dawn.
We watched the lean branches grow,
And through the days of seasonless years
We nursed the infant leaves.
From the angry element we shielded the bud,
And against all dark spirits we guarded the flower.
And now that our vine hath yielded the grape
You will not take it to the winepress and fill the
    cup.

10

Whose mightier hand than yours shall reap the
fruit?
And what nobler end than your thirst awaits the
wine?
Man is food for the gods,
And the glory of man begins
When his aimless breath is sucked by gods' hal-
lowed lips.
All that is human counts for naught if human it re-
main;
The innocence of childhood, and the sweet ecstasy
of youth,
The passion of stern manhood, and the wisdom of
old age;
The splendor of kings and the triumph of warriors,
The fame of poets and the honor of dreamers and
saints;
All these and all that lieth therein is bred for gods.
And naught but bread ungraced shall it be
If the gods raise it not to their mouths.
And as the mute grain turns to love songs when

11

swallowed by the nightingale,
Even so as bread for gods shall man taste godhead.

Aye, man is meat for gods!
And all that is man shall come upon the gods' eter-
   nal board!
The pain of child-bearing and the agony of child-
   birth,
The blind cry of the infant that pierces the naked
   night,
And the anguish of the mother wrestling with the
   sleep she craves,
To pour life exhausted from her breast;
The flaming breath of youth tormented,
And the burdened sobs of passion unspent;
The dripping brows of manhood tilling the barren
   land,
And the regret of pale old age when life against
   life's will
Calls to the grave.

12

Behold this is man!
A creature bred on hunger and made food for hun-
    gry gods.
A vine that creeps in dust beneath the feet of death-
    less death.
The flower that blooms in nights of evil shadows;
The grape of mournful days, and days of terror and
    shame.
And yet you would have me eat and drink.
You would bid me sit amongst shrouded faces
And draw my life from stony lips
And from withered hands receive my eternity.

THIRD GOD

Brothers, my dreaded brothers,
Thrice deep the youth is singing,
And thrice higher is his song.
His voice shakes the forest
And pierces the sky,
And scatters the slumbering of earth.

SECOND GOD (*Always unhearing*)

The bee hums harshly in your ears,
And foul is the honey to your lips.
Fain would I comfort you,
But how shall I?
Only the abyss listens when gods call unto gods,
For measureless is the gulf that lies between divini-
    ties,
And windless is the space.
Yet I would comfort you,
I would make serene your clouded sphere;
And though equal we are in power and judgment,
I would counsel you.

⁻ When out of chaos came the earth, and we, sons
of the beginning, beheld each other in the lustless
light, we breathed the first hushed, tremulous sound
that quickened the currents of air and sea.

Then we walked, hand in hand, upon the gray infant world, and out of the echoes of our first drowsy
steps time was born, a fourth divinity, that sets his

feet upon our footprints, shadowing our thoughts and desires, and seeing only with our eyes.

And unto earth came life, and unto life came the spirit, the winged melody of the universe. And we ruled life and spirit, and none save us knew the measure of the years nor the weight of years' nebulous dreams, till we, at noontide of the seventh æon, gave the sea in marriage to the sun.

And from the inner chamber of their nuptial ecstasy, we brought man, a creature who, though yielding and infirm, bears ever the marks of his parentage.

Through man who walks earth with eyes upon the stars, we find pathways to earth's distant regions; and of man, the humble reed growing beside dark waters, we make a flute through whose hollowed heart we pour our voice to the silence-bound world. From the sunless north to the sun-smitten sand of
the south.
From the lotus land where days are born
To perilous isles where days are slain,

Man, the faint hearted, overbold by our purpose,
Ventures with lyre and sword.
Ours is the will he heralds,
And our the sovereignty he proclaims,
And his love trodden courses are rivers, to the sea of
    our desires.
We, upon the heights, in man's sleep dream our
    dreams.
We urge his days to part from the valley of twilights
And seek their fullness upon the hills.
Our hands direct the tempests that sweep the world
And summon man from sterile peace to fertile strife,
And on to triumph.
In our eyes is the vision that turns man's soul to
    flame,
And leads him to exalted loneliness and rebellious
    prophecy,
And on to crucifixion.
Man is born to bondage,
And in bondage is his honor and his reward.
In man we seek a mouthpiece,

16

And in his life our self fulfillment.
Whose heart shall echo our voice if the human heart
    is deafened with dust?
Who shall behold our shining if man's eye is blinded
    with night?
And what would you do with man, child of our
    earliest heart, our own self image?

THIRD GOD

Brothers, my mighty brothers,
The dancer's feet are drunk with songs.
They set the air a-throbbing,
And like doves her hands fly upward.

FIRST GOD

The lark calls to the lark,
But upward the eagle soars,
Nor tarries to hear the song.
You would teach me self love fulfilled in man's
    worship,
And content with man's servitude.

But my self love is limitless and without measure.
I would rise beyond my earthbound mortality
And throne me upon the heavens.
My arms would girdle space and encompass the
    spheres.
I would take the starry way for a bow,
And the comets for arrows,
And with the infinite would I conquer the infinite.

But you would not do this, were it in your power.
For even as man is to man,
So are gods to gods.
Nay, you would bring to my weary heart
Remembrance of cycles spent in mist,
When my soul sought itself among the mountains
And mine eyes pursued their own image in slumber-
    ing waters;
Though my yesterday died in child-birth
And only silence visits her womb,
And the wind strewn sand nestles at her breast.
18

Oh yesterday, dead yesterday,
Mother of my chained divinity,
What super-god caught you in your flight
And made you breed in the cage?
What giant sun warmed your bosom
To give me birth?
I bless you not, yet I would not curse you;
For even as you have burdened me with life
So I have burdened man.
But less cruel have I been.
I, immortal, made man a passing shadow;
And you, dying, conceived me deathless.

Yesterday, dead yesterday,
Shall you return with distant tomorrow,
That I may bring you to judgment?
And will you wake with life's second dawn
That I may erase your earth-clinging memory from
    the earth?
Would that you might rise with all the dead of yore,
Till the land choke with its own bitter fruit,

19

And all the seas be stagnant with the slain,
And woe upon woe exhaust earth's vain fertility.

THIRD GOD

Brother, my sacred brothers,
The girl has heard the song,
And now she seeks the singer.
Like a fawn in glad surprise
She leaps over rocks and streams
And turns her to every side.
Oh, the joy in mortal intent,
The eye of purpose half-born;
The smile on lips that quiver
With foretaste of promised delight!
What flower has fallen from heaven,
What flame has risen from hell,
That startled the heart of silence
To this breathless joy and fear?
What dream dreamt we upon the height,
What thought gave we to the wind
That woke the drowsing valley
And made watchful the night?

20

SECOND GOD

The sacred loom is given you,
And the art to weave the fabric.
The loom and the art shall be yours forevermore,
And yours the dark thread and the light,
And yours the purple and the gold.
Yet you would grudge yourself a raiment.
Your hands have spun man's soul
From living air and fire,
Yet now you would break the thread,
And lend your versèd fingers to an idle eternity.

FIRST GOD

Nay, unto eternity unmoulded I would give my
    hands,
And to untrodden fields assign my feet.
What joy is there in songs oft heard,
Whose tune the remembering ear arrests
Ere the breath yields it to the wind?
My heart longs for what my heart conceives not,

21

And unto the unknown where memory dwells not
I would command my spirit.
Oh, tempt me not with glory possessed,
And seek not to comfort me with your dream or
    mine,
For all that I am, and all that there is on earth,
And all that shall be, inviteth not my soul.
    Oh my soul,
    Silent is thy face,
    And in thine eyes the shadows of night are sleep-
        ing.
    But terrible is thy silence,
    And thou art terrible.

THIRD GOD

Brothers, my solemn brothers,
The girl has found the singer.
She sees his raptured face.
Panther-like she slips with subtle steps
Through rustling vine and fern.
And now amid his ardent cries

22

He gazes full on her.

Oh my brothers, my heedless brothers,
Is it some other god in passion
Who has woven this web of scarlet and white?
What unbridled star has gone astray?
Whose secret keepeth night from morning?
And whose hand is upon our world?

FIRST GOD

Oh my soul, my soul,
Thou burning sphere that girdles me,
How shall I guide thy course,
And unto what space direct thy eagerness?

Oh my mateless soul,
In thy hunger thou preyest upon thyself,
And with thine own tears thou wouldst quench thy
    thirst;
For night gathers not her dew into thy cup,
And the day brings thee no fruit.

23

Oh my soul, my soul,
Thou grounded ship laden with desire,
Whence shall come the wind to fill thy sail,
And what higher tide shall release thy rudder?
Weighed is thine anchor and thy wings would
    spread,
But the skies are silent above thee,
And the still sea mocks at thy immobility.

And what hope is there for thee and me?
What shifting of worlds, what new purpose in the
    heavens,
That shall claim thee?
Does the womb of the virgin infinite
Bear the seed of thy Redeemer,
One mightier than thy vision
Whose hand shall deliver thee from thy captivity?

SECOND GOD

Hold your importunate cry,
And the breath of your burning heart,

24

For deaf is the ear of the infinite,
And heedless is the sky.
We are the beyond and we are the Most High,
And between us and boundless eternity
Is naught save our unshaped passion
And the motive thereof.

You invoke the unknown,
And the unknown clad with moving mist
Dwells in your own soul.
Yea, in your own soul your Redeemer lies asleep,
And in sleep sees what your waking eye does not see.
And that is the secret of our being.
Would you leave the harvest ungathered,
In haste to sow again the dreaming furrow?
And wherefore spread you your cloud in trackless
        fields and desolate,
When your own flock is seeking you,
And would fain gather in your shadow?
Forbear and look down upon the world.
Behold the unweaned children of your love.

The earth is your abode, and the earth is your
  throne;
And high beyond man's furtherest hope
Your hand upholds his destiny.
You would not abandon him
Who strives to reach you through gladness and
  through pain.
You would not turn away your face from the need
  in his eye.

FIRST GOD

Does dawn hold the heart of night unto her heart?
Or shall the sea heed the bodies of her dead?
Like dawn my soul rises within me
Naked and unencumbered.
And like the unresting sea
My heart casts out a perishing wrack of man and
  earth.
I would not cling to that that clings to me.
But unto that that rises beyond my reach I would
  arise.

26

Brothers, behold, my brothers,
They meet, two star-bound spirits in the sky en-
    countering.
In silence they gaze the one upon the other.
He sings no more,
And yet his sunburnt throat throbs with the song;
And in her limbs the happy dance is stayed
But not asleep.

Brothers, my strange brothers,
The night waxeth deep,
And brighter is the moon,
And twixt the meadow and the sea
A voice in rapture calleth you and me.

SECOND GOD

To be, to rise, to burn before the burning sun,
To live, and to watch the nights of the living
As Orion watches us!

To face the four winds with a head crowned and
 high,
And to heal the ills of man with our tideless breath!
The tentmaker sits darkly at his loom,
And the potter turns his wheel unaware;
But we, the sleepless and the knowing,
We are released from guessing and from chance.
We pause not nor do we wait for thought.
We are beyond all restless questioning.
Be content and let the dreaming go.
Like rivers let us flow to ocean
Unwounded by the edges of the rocks;
And when we reach her heart and are merged,
No more shall we wrangle and reason of tomorrow.

FIRST GOD

Oh, this ache of ceaseless divining,
This vigil of guiding the day unto twilight,
And the night unto dawn;
This tide of ever remembering and forgetting;
This ever sowing destinies and reaping but hopes;

28

This changeless lifting of self from dust to mist,
Only to long for dust, and to fall down with long-
    ing unto dust,
And still with greater longing to seek the mist again.
And this timeless measuring of time.
Must my soul needs to be a sea whose currents for-
    ever confound one another,
Or the sky where the warring winds turn hurricane?

Were I man, a blind fragment,
I could have met it with patience.
Or if I were the Supreme Godhead,
Who fills the emptiness of man and of gods,
I would be fulfilled.
But you and I are neither human,
Nor the Supreme above us.
We are but twilights ever rising and ever fading
Between horizon and horizon.
We are but gods holding a world and held by it,
Fates that sound the trumpets
Whilst the breath and the music come from beyond.

29

And I rebel.
I would exhaust myself to emptiness.
I would dissolve myself afar from your vision,
And from the memory of this silent youth, our
    younger brother,
Who sits beside us gazing into yonder valley,
And though his lips move, utters not a word.

THIRD GOD

I speak, my unheeding brothers,
I do indeed speak,
But you hear only your own words.
I bid you see your glory and mine,
But you turn, and close your eyes,
And rock your thrones.
Ye sovereigns who would govern the above world
    and the world beneath,
Gods self-bent, whose yesterday is ever jealous of
    your tomorrow,
Self-weary, who would unleash your temper with
    speech

And lash our orb with thunderings!
Your feud is but the sounding of an Ancient Lyre
Whose strings have been half forgotten by His
    fingers
Who has Orion for a harp and the Pleiades for
    cymbals.
Even now, while you are muttering and rumbling,
His harp rings, His cymbals clash,
And I beseech you hear His song.

   Behold, man and woman,
   Flame to flame,
   In white ecstasy.
Roots that suck at the breast of purple earth,
Flame flowers at the breasts of the sky.
And we are the purple breast,
And we are the enduring sky.
Our soul, even the soul of life, your soul and mine,
Dwells this night in a throat enflamed,
And garments the body of a girl with beating waves.
Your sceptre cannot sway this destiny,

Your weariness is but ambition.
This and all is wiped away
In the passion of a man and a maid.

Yea, what of this love of man and woman?
See how the east wind dances with her dancing feet,
And the west wind rises singing with his song.
Behold our sacred purpose now enthroned,
In the yielding of a spirit that sings to a body that
    dances.

I will not turn my eyes downward to the conceit of
    earth,
Nor to her children in their slow agony that you call
    love.
And what is love,
But the muffled drum and leads the long procession
    of sweet uncertainty
To another slow agony?
I will not look downward.

32

What is there to behold
Save a man and a woman in the forest that grew to
    trap them
That they might renounce self
And parent creatures for our unborn tomorrow?

THIRD GOD

Oh, the affliction of knowing,
The starless veil of prying and questioning
Which we have laid upon the world;
And the challenge to human forbearance!
We would lay under a stone a waxen shape
And say, It is a thing of clay,
And in clay let it find its end.
We would hold in our hands a white flame
And say in our heart,
It is a fragment of ourselves returning,
A breath of our breath that had escaped,
And now haunts our hands and lips for more fra-
    grance.
Earth gods, my brothers,

High upon the mountain,
We are still earth-bound,
Through man desiring the golden hours of man's
    destiny.
Shall our wisdom ravish beauty from his eyes?
Shall our measures subdue his passion to stillness,
Or to our own passion?

What would your armies of reasoning
Where love encamps his host?
They who are conquered by love,
And upon whose bodies love's chariot ran
From sea to mountain
And again from mountain to the sea,
Stand even now in a shy half-embrace.
Petal unto petal they breathe the sacred perfume,
Soul to soul they find the soul of life,
And upon their eyelids lies a prayer
Unto you and unto me.
Love is a night bent down to a bower anointed,
A sky turned meadow, and all the stars to fireflies.

34

True it is, we are the beyond,
And we are the most high.
But love is beyond our questioning,
And love outsoars our song.

SECOND GOD

Seek you a distant orb,
And would not consider this star
Where your sinews are planted?
There is no centre in space
Save where self is wedded to self,
And beauty is the witness and the priest.
And see and behold beauty scattered about our feet,
And beauty filling our hands to shame our lips.
The most distant is the most near.
And where beauty is, there are all things.

Oh, lofty dreaming brother,
Return to us from time's dim borderland!
Unlace your feet from no-where and no-when,
And dwell with us in this security

35

Which your hand interwined with ours
Has builded stone upon stone.
Cast off your mantle of brooding,
And comrade us, masters of the young earth green
    and warm.

FIRST GOD

Eternal Altar! Wouldst thou indeed this night
A god for sacrifice?
Now then, I come, and coming I offer up
My passion and my pain.
Lo, there is the dancer, carved out of our ancient
    eagerness,
And the singer is crying mine own songs unto the
    wind.
And in that dancing and in that singing
A god is slain within me.
My god-heart within my human ribs
Shouts to my god-heart in mid-air.
The human pit that wearied me calls to divinity.
36

The beauty that we have sought from the begin-
    ning
Calls unto divinity.
I heed, and I have measured the call,
And now I yield.
Beauty is a path that leads to self self-slain.
Beat your strings.
I will to walk the path.
It stretches ever to another dawn.

THIRD GOD

Love triumphs.
The white and green of love beside a lake,
And the proud majesty of love in tower or balcony;
Love in a garden or in the desert untrodden,
Love is our lord and master.
It is not a wanton decay of the flesh,
Nor the crumbling of desire
When desire and self are wrestling;
Nor is it flesh that takes arms against the spirit.
Love rebels not.

It only leaves the trodden way of ancient destinies
    for the sacred grove,
To sing and dance its secret to eternity.
Love is youth with chains broken,
Manhood made free from the sod,
And womanhood warmed by the flame
And shining with the light of heaven deeper than
    our heaven.
Love is a distant laughter in the spirit.
It is a wild assault that hushes you to your awaken-
    ing.
It is a new dawn upon the earth,
A day not yet achieved in your eyes or mine,
But already achieved in its own greater heart.

Brothers, my brothers,
The bride comes from the heart of dawn,
And the bridegroom from the sunset.
There is a wedding in the valley.
A day too vast for recording.

38

Thus has it been since the first morn
Discharged the plains to hill and vale,
And thus shall it be to the last even-tide.
Our roots have brought forth the dancing branches
      in the valley,
And we are the flowering of the song-scent that rises
      to the heights.
Immortal and mortal, twin rivers calling to the sea.
There is no emptiness between call and call,
But only in the ear.
Time maketh our listening more certain,
And giveth it more desire.
Only doubt in mortal hushes the sound.
We have outsoared the doubt.
Man is a child of our younger heart.
Man is god in slow arising;
And betwixt his joy and his pain
Lies our sleeping, and the dreaming thereof.

FIRST GOD

Let the singer cry, and let the dancer whirl her feet
And let me be content awhile.
Let my soul be serene this night.
Perchance I may drowse, and drowsing
Behold a brighter world
And creatures more starry supple to my mind.

THIRD GOD

Now I will rise and strip me of time and space,
And I will dance in that field untrodden,
And the dancer's feet will move with my feet;
And I will sing in that higher air,
And a human voice will throb within my voice.

We shall pass into the twilight;
Perchance to wake to the dawn of another world.
But love shall stay,
And his finger-marks shall not be erased.

The blessed forge burns,

40

The sparks rise, and each spark is a sun.
Better it is for us, and wiser,
To seek a shadowed nook and sleep in our earth
    divinity,
And let love, human and frail, command the com-
    ing day.

A NOTE ON THE AUTHOR

KAHLIL GIBRAN, poet, philosopher, and artist, was born in 1883 into an affluent and musical Lebanese family. He was a college student in Syria at the age of fifteen, studied art in Paris at the Ecole des Beaux Arts, and had visited America twice before he came to New York to stay in 1912 and adopted English as his literary language. He died in New York City's Greenwich Village on April 10, 1931.

His drawings and paintings have been exhibited in the great capitals of the world and were compared by Auguste Rodin to the work of William Blake. *The Prophet*, his most popular book, published in 1923, has been translated into more than twenty languages, and has sold well over a million copies in this country alone.

This book was set on the linotype in Original Old Style. Of the history of this type very little is known; in practically its present form, it has been used for many years for fine book and magazine work. Original Old Style possesses in a high degree those two qualities by which a book type must be judged: first, legibility, and second, the ability to impart a definite character to a page without intruding itself upon the reader's consciousness.

PRINTED AND BOUND BY THE BOOK PRESS,
BRATTLEBORO, VERMONT